83 low-cholesterol recipes

COOKING
FOR A
HEALTHY HEART

JACQUI MORRELL

HAMLYN HEALTHY EATING

This book is for my Dad who is a 'great cooker'!

An Hachette UK Company
www.hachette.co.uk

First published in Great Britain in 2002 by
Hamlyn, a division of Octopus Publishing Group Ltd
Endeavour House
189 Shaftesbury Avenue
London
WC2H 8JY
www.octopusbooksusa.com

Revised editions 2004 and 2009
This edition published in 2014

Distributed in the US by
Hachette Book Group USA
237 Park Avenue
New York NY 10017 USA

Distributed in Canada by
Canadian Manda Group
165 Dufferin Street
Toronto, Ontario, Canada M6K 3H6

ISBN 978-0-600-62878-1

Printed and bound in China

10 9 8 7 6 5 4 3 2 1

The publisher has taken all reasonable care in the preparation of this book but the information it contains is not intended to take the place of treatment by a qualified medical practitioner.

NOTES

A few recipes include nuts and nut derivatives. Anyone with a known nut allergy must avoid these.

Cage-free medium eggs should be used unless otherwise stated. The U.S. Food and Drug Administration advises that eggs should not be consumed raw. This book contains some dishes made with raw or lightly cooked eggs. It is prudent for vulnerable people, such as pregnant and nursing mothers, people with weakened immune systems, the elderly, babies, and young children, to avoid uncooked or lightly cooked dishes made with eggs. Once prepared, these dishes should be kept refrigerated and used promptly.

Meat and poultry should be cooked thoroughly. To test if poultry is cooked, pierce the flesh through the thickest part with a skewer or fork—the juices should run clear, never pink or red.

All the recipes in this book have been analyzed by the author. The analysis refers to each serving, unless otherwise stated.

Contents

Introduction

Heart disease is now established as the number one killer in the world, claiming more than six million people each year. Nearly all deaths from heart disease are as a result of a heart attack or "myocardial infarction." About half of all heart attacks are fatal, and in about a third of them death occurs before reaching the hospital. In the USA, heart disease will claim a victim every single minute. Many deaths are premature, and family, friends, and colleagues are all affected by the tragedy. For those who are lucky enough to survive a heart attack, life is never quite the same again. Heart disease has developed into a lethal epidemic and the problem is set to continue since people now live longer and many people also have unhealthy lifestyles.

Yet heart disease is potentially avoidable and preventable. If you want to beat heart disease, rethinking your lifestyle can help reduce many of the risk factors of heart disease such as high cholesterol, high blood pressure, diabetes, smoking, and being overweight. If you already have heart disease, it is never too late to re-evaluate your lifestyle, and there is overwhelming evidence that changing your eating habits can save your life.

Dietary advice can be all too confusing, given that we are being bombarded by often conflicting messages, but that is because the effect of diet is complex and there is still much to discover. Simply advocating a low-fat diet is no longer adequate, and current interest is focused on the benefits of a broad-based, multi-faceted dietary approach. This book clearly and concisely explains the latest dietary advice from medical and nutritional experts to help you eat for a healthy heart, and its recommendations are based on consensus opinion and sound scientific research.

How Your Heart Works

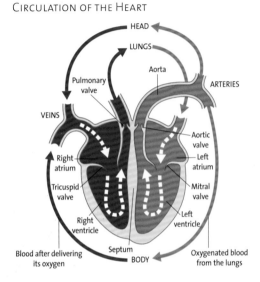

HEAD
LUNGS
Aorta
Pulmonary valve
ARTERIES
VEINS
Aortic valve
Right atrium
Left atrium
Tricuspid valve
Mitral valve
Right ventricle
Left ventricle
Blood after delivering its oxygen
Septum
BODY
Oxygenated blood from the lungs

CORONARY ARTERIES AROUND THE HEART

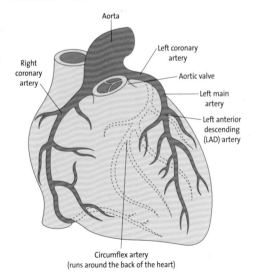

Aorta
Right coronary artery
Left coronary artery
Aortic valve
Left main artery
Left anterior descending (LAD) artery
Circumflex artery
(runs around the back of the heart)

A Strong Heart for a Long Life

The heart is the powerhouse of the body, driving blood to all the organs in your body. It is an enormously strong muscle and is about the size of a clenched fist. It beats tirelessly, 60 to 80 times a minute (and more if you do anything energetic), day and night, pumping out between 10 and 42 pints of blood every minute, depending on your body's needs.

We feel each heartbeat or contraction of the heart muscle as the pulse. The medical term for this contraction is systole. Diastole describes the relaxation of the heart between beats. The heart has two pairs of chambers, two on the right and two on the left. The right half of the heart pumps blood through the lungs to pick up oxygen, and the left half of the heart pumps oxygen-rich blood, returning from the lungs, to the rest of the body.

Coronary Arteries

To do all this work, the heart muscle itself needs fuel and oxygen for energy, and it gets this from its own blood supply. The blood vessels that supply the heart are called coronary arteries. They need to be tough to cope with the pressure of the beating heart.

Physical Fitness

The size of the heart and how efficiently it beats depend upon your physical fitness. People who exercise regularly have larger, stronger hearts that beat more slowly to deliver the same amount of blood as the heart of a less fit person. You can lower your pulse rate by increasing your exercise levels—ideally, brisk walking for 30 minutes on most days of the week.

What is Heart Disease?

Coronary heart disease (angina and heart attack) occurs when the coronary arteries become narrower or blocked due to aging, poor diet, and an unhealthy lifestyle. Tragically, the process can even begin in childhood. The narrowing of the arteries is due to fatty deposits forming in the smooth artery lining and is called atherosclerosis.

Angina

Narrowed coronary arteries reduce the rate at which blood can be delivered to the beating heart muscle. The muscle doesn't get enough oxygen to fuel the work it is doing and signals this with the pain of angina. Angina is usually felt across the front of the chest but sometimes in the shoulders, arms, throat, or jaw. It is usually a heavy or tight pain, generally lasting less than ten minutes.

Heart Attack

A heart attack occurs when a coronary artery becomes entirely blocked due to the combination of atherosclerosis and the sudden development of a blood clot. The sudden blockage of the artery means that the part of the heart muscle that was supplied by that coronary artery is at once deprived of blood and oxygen. Muscle cannot survive without blood, so the affected area of the heart muscle dies and the pain is more intense and lasts longer than with angina.

Cholesterol

Cholesterol, a white waxy substance, is vital for the human body since it forms cell membranes, various hormones, bile salts, and vitamin D. However, an excess of cholesterol in the blood can increase your risk of heart disease. A number of factors affect your blood cholesterol levels. Most cholesterol is made in the liver, but some is absorbed from food by the digestive system. Foods high in saturated fat, such as fatty meats, eggs, butter, cheese, whole milk, cream, and most cakes, increase your blood cholesterol levels.

Cholesterol travels to your body's cells through the bloodstream in tiny packages called lipoproteins. Scientists distinguish the types of packages by their density, and the most important types are low-density lipoprotein cholesterol (LDL cholesterol) and high-density

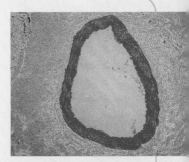

ABOVE: A healthy human coronary artery which is found on the surface of the heart and supplies blood to the heart muscle. The heart muscle is colored blue in this example. The artery wall is colored red.

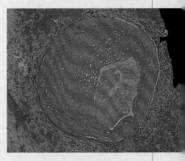

ABOVE: A blocked human artery. The coronary artery (colored red) lies on the surface of the heart. The narrowed, light brown channel is blocked by a clot and the loss of blood supply to the heart muscle has resulted in a fatal heart attack.

Above: Fruit and vegetables rich in antioxidant nutrients protect LDL cholesterol from oxidation.

Assessing and Reducing Risk Factors

There are a number of factors that influence the incidence of heart disease.

Factors That Can Be Reduced or Eliminated

High blood cholesterol levels
High blood pressure
Smoking
Diabetes
Being overweight
Lack of physical activity

Factors That You Cannot Change

♥ Age – the older you are, the greater the risk
♥ Gender – women before the menopause are at lower risk of heart disease than men
♥ Family history – you are at increased risk if there is heart disease in your family, especially in a close relative under 55

lipoprotein cholesterol (HDL cholesterol). Most of the blood cholesterol is carried as LDL cholesterol from the liver to other parts of the body.

Having a high level of LDL cholesterol increases your risk of heart disease because when oxidized, it can slowly build up in the walls of coronary arteries and ultimately cause a heart attack. Therefore, your target level of LDL cholesterol should be below 195 mg/dl (3.0 mmol/l).

HDL cholesterol acts as an arterial scavenger, carrying cholesterol away from body tissues, including artery walls, back to the liver. The higher the HDL cholesterol level, the lower your risk of heart disease. Your target level should be above 35 mg/dl (0.9 mmol/l).

High Blood Pressure

If your blood pressure is constantly above 140/90 mmHg, you have high blood pressure or hypertension. This adds to the workload of your heart and arteries. The heart must work harder than normal and this may cause it to enlarge. As you grow older, your arteries will harden and become less elastic, and high blood pressure speeds up this process. It can be controlled by a combination of healthy eating, physical activity, and medication.

People at Risk

People with diabetes are at high risk of heart disease and should pay particular attention to the risk factors, follow a healthy lifestyle, and use appropriate drug therapy. Smoking cigarettes and other tobacco products also raises the risk of heart attack and stroke. Even passive smoking significantly increases the risk of heart disease.

Physical Activity

Physical activity helps prevent and treat heart disease as well as other major risk factors such as high blood pressure and high blood cholesterol. Medical studies have shown that just getting our bodies moving every day can have long-term health benefits.

The physical activity needs to be regular, of moderate intensity, and aerobic. Aerobic exercise is any activity in which the large muscles in the arms or legs are moving rhythmically such as brisk walking, dancing, or cycling. Even taking the stairs more often or parking your car further away from your destination can help increase your activity levels. Try to do at least 30 minutes of these activities on most days, and if you don't have 30 minutes to spare, try to do 15 minutes twice or ten minutes three times a day. Pick activities that are fun, that suit your needs, and that you can do all year round.

The Disease–Diet Link

There is a wealth of information that links diet and the risk of heart disease. The emerging picture is that we should adopt a pattern of eating that can protect against heart disease. But there is no single individual dietary intervention that will guard you against heart disease, and you must look to make several changes to maximize the cardio-protective potential of what you eat.

The classic Seven Countries Study led by Ancel Keys in the 1960s showed a link between saturated fat intake and rate of heart disease in seven different countries. Keys showed that in Japan and the rural Mediterranean countries of southern Europe such as Greece and Italy, where the intake of saturated fat from meat and dairy products was low, there were significantly lower rates of heart disease than in the UK and the USA, where intakes of saturated fat were higher.

The Mediterranean Diet

The characteristic Mediterranean diet is high in fruit, vegetables, bread and other forms of cereals, potatoes, beans, nuts, and seeds. It features olive oil as an important fat source, while dairy products, fish, poultry, and eggs are consumed in low to moderate amounts. Only a little red meat is eaten, but a glass or two of wine compensates!

OLIVE OIL

Olive oil contains mainly monounsaturated fat (see page 13) and, when used to replace saturated fat in the diet, lowers total and LDL cholesterol without decreasing the "good guy" HDL cholesterol. Substituting saturated fat with high levels of polyunsaturated fat or carbohydrates can produce the undesirable effect of decreasing HDL cholesterol.

FRUIT AND VEGETABLES

Another significant factor is that the Mediterranean-style diet is high in fruit and vegetables, which are rich in vitamins and minerals, essential fatty acids, and antioxidants. There are about 600 antioxidants and these include the ACE vitamins, minerals, and various other compounds that give fruit and vegetables their fabulous colors. Red wine and tea are also known to be good sources of antioxidants. The antioxidants protect LDL cholesterol from becoming oxidized, which makes it more toxic and more likely to accumulate in the artery walls. Fruit and vegetables also supply other protective nutrients. For example, folic acid is found in dark green vegetables, fruit, and whole grains, and helps to maintain lower levels of homocysteine in the blood. High levels of homocysteine are linked to an increased risk of heart disease.

ABOVE: Mediterranean lifestyle has long been known to be healthy. We now know that an abundance of fresh fruit, vegetables, and olive oil play a significant part.

The Lyon Diet Heart Study, carried out in France by A. Lorgeril *et al.* and first published in 1994, provided evidence that if you adopt a Mediterranean-style diet after you have a heart attack, you can expect a dramatic reduction in the risk of another heart attack.

The Benefits of Soybeans

In Asian countries, with traditionally high intakes of soybean products, there is far less cardiovascular disease. Soybeans contain phytoestrogens, naturally occurring compounds that are structurally similar to estrogen. In addition, isoflavones in soy products exert a favorable effect on the lining of blood vessels and improve vascular tone.

The Benefits of Omega-3

Fish can play a huge part in preventing heart disease. People who eat fish and shellfish regularly, such as the Japanese and Greenland Inuits, have fewer heart attacks than non-fish eaters. Oily fish is the richest source of the polyunsaturated fatty acids—eicosapentanoic acid (EPA) and docosahexanoic Acid (DHA), or omega-3 fatty acids.

ABOVE: Countries that consume a lot of soybeans also have lower levels of cardiovascular disease due to the phytoestrogens in beans.

Omega-3 fatty acids are also found in seed oils, soy, nuts, and green vegetables, and can play an important part in blood-clotting mechanisms, making the blood less sticky and reducing the risk of thrombosis.

Popping Pills Versus Real Food

Recent well-designed clinical trials (MRC/BHF Heart Protection Study, R. Collins, (UK), published 2002; GISSI study, R. Marchioli, (Italy), published 1999) have confirmed that there seems little benefit in taking individual nutrients such as vitamin E, C, or beta-carotene in supplement form as vitamin preparations. This would suggest that the benefit may only occur when the antioxidants are taken as part of a healthy eating pattern, containing plenty of whole foods, including fruit and vegetables. However, if you can't eat fish, or don't like it, it is a good idea to take a supplement of omega-3 fatty acids (EPA and DHA) in capsule form, at 1 g per day.

Shaping Up

The shape you are has a link with heart disease. If you are apple-shaped, where fat is deposited around your stomach, you are at greater risk of heart disease than if you are pear-shaped, with fat distributed over your hips and thighs. This is because fat cells over the stomach make the body more resistant to the hormone insulin. To compensate, more insulin is produced, which increases blood pressure, cholesterol, and triglycerides, lowers HDL cholesterol, and increases the tendency for the blood to form clots. And, of course, your risk of becoming diabetic is increased. This clustering of risk factors is called the Insulin Resistance Syndrome.

By keeping to foods with a low glycemic index (GI), you are less likely to develop insulin resistance, diabetes, and heart disease. GI is a measurement of the effects of carbohydrate-rich foods on blood glucose levels. Starchy foods that take a long time to be digested and absorbed have a low GI, and have a favorable effect on blood glucose and insulin.

Top Ten Tips for Healthy Living

1 Enjoy a Wide Variety of Nutritious Foods

Eat a combination of different foods, which will help give you all the essential nutrients in balanced proportions. Try to adopt the Mediterranean diet most of the time (see page 9). This should be a lifelong approach, not just a five-minute wonder, so make it easy for yourself by making simple changes one at a time. Above all, enjoy your food!

2 Be a Healthy Weight for Your Height

Make sure you keep to a healthy weight for your height by monitoring your waist measurement.

You should aim to keep your waist circumference in the healthy range—less than 37 inches for men and 32 inches for women. If your waist measurement is more than this, try to lose weight by reducing your calorie intake to less than your body uses and increase your physical activity at the same time.

3 Eat Plenty of Fruit, Vegetables, and Salads

You should eat at least five portions a day. An easy tip to remember is that a portion of fruit or vegetables is about the size of a clenched fist, and that five portions should add up to about a pound in weight.

PORTION GUIDE
- ❤ 1 large fruit (such as an apple, orange, or banana)
- ❤ 2 small fruits (such as plums or clementines)
- ❤ 1 cup of raspberries, strawberries, or grapes
- ❤ 1 glass ($^2/_3$ cup) of fruit juice
- ❤ 1 tablespoon of dried fruit
- ❤ 2 tablespoons of raw, cooked, or frozen vegetables
- ❤ 1 dessert bowl of salad

4 Eat Fish Two or Three Times a Week

Eat more fish, particularly oily fish, especially if you have already had a heart attack. Oily fish are the richest source of omega-3 fatty acids. If you can't eat fish, you should take a daily

Waist Measurements

Men
37–40 inches:
you are overweight
Over 40 inches:
you are fat

Women
32–35 inches:
you are overweight
Over 35 inches:
you are fat

❤ Measure with a tape measure next to your skin, not over your clothes
❤ Make sure the tape is level at the navel
❤ Let the tape fit around your waist—don't pull too tightly
❤ Try to measure in the same place each time

supplement of 1 g of omega-3 fatty acids. Look out for a special variety of eggs that contain omega-3, produced by chickens that have been fed an omega-3-packed diet.

Top Fish Sources of Omega-3

	(omega-3 per portion)
Mackerel	4.5 g
Pilchards (canned in tomato sauce)	3.2 g
Trout	2.9 g
Salmon	2.5 g
Herring	2.2 g
Sardines (canned in tomato sauce)	2.0 g
Salmon (canned)	1.9 g
Crab (canned)	0.9 g

Top Plant Sources of Omega-3

	(omega-3 per portion)
Flaxseed and flaxseed oil (linseeds and linseed oil)	1.8 g
Walnuts and walnut oil	1.5 g
Sweet potatoes and pumpkins	1.3 g
Rapeseed oil (canola oil)	1.1 g
Soybean oil	0.8 g
Spinach and leafy green vegetables	0.2 g

ABOVE: Stick to the advice in Tip 4 to ensure that your diet is getting an optimum amount of omega-3 fatty acids. If you do not eat fish, there are plenty of plant sources that will also provide enough amounts.

5 Base Meals and Snacks Around Wholegrain Foods

Wholegrain foods include bread, cereals, rice, pasta, and starchy food, such as potatoes. They are filling yet not fattening, and are great sources of fiber, both soluble and insoluble.

♥ Sources of fiber

Soluble – lowers cholesterol

Oats – rolled oats, oat bran, oat-based cereals, and breads

Beans – peas, split peas, lentils, chickpeas, soybeans, and baked beans

Some fruits – apples, strawberries, and citrus fruits

Insoluble – prevents bowel problems

Wholegrain bread and cereals

Brown rice

Wholewheat pasta

Fruit and vegetables

6 Eat a Diet Low in Fat

There are three main types of fat in food—saturated, monounsaturated, and polyunsaturated.

❤ SATURATED FATS
Found in: Fatty meats, full-cream dairy products such as milk, cream, and cheese, coconut and palm oil used in convenience foods, cakes, pastries, cookies, certain candies, many pre-packed foods, and take-out meals.
Effect: Raise cholesterol

❤ TRANS FATS
Found in: Small amounts in the fat of dairy products and some meats but mainly in hydrogenated vegetable oils, some margarines, and in many commercially prepared foods such as cookies, pastries, cakes, and other desserts and baked goods.
Effect: Raise cholesterol

ABOVE: If you want to use a spread, choose a low-fat version made from vegetable oils that will help you to lower your cholesterol.

❤ POLYUNSATURATED FATS
Found in: Vegetable oils such as sunflower, corn, safflower, and soy, grapeseed and nut oils, and many margarines and spreads contain omega-6 polyunsaturated fatty acids. Vegetables and fish oils contain omega-3 fatty acids.
Effect: Lower cholesterol

❤ MONOUNSATURATED FATS
Found in: Olive and rapeseed (canola) oil, peanut oil and spreads, avocados, and nuts.
Effect: Lower cholesterol

You should avoid saturated fat and choose fats that are unsaturated, particularly olive oil and rapeseed (canola) oil. Rapeseed oil is a good source of omega-3 fatty acids and is increasingly the chosen oil for most unspecified vegetable oils, but always check the label.

HOW MUCH FAT SHOULD YOU EAT IN A DAY?

A healthy fat intake is based on your energy needs and activity levels. An average man may require 2,500 calories per day and an average woman, 2,000 calories per day. You need to limit

ABOVE: Experiment with the oil-water spray when grilling—try it on lean pork steaks for example, and accompany with steamed vegetables for an ultra healthy supper.

your total fat intake so that no more than 35 percent of your total calories come from fat.

If you need to lose weight, you should reduce your entire fat intake and this means even the good fats, since all fat is fattening! Use low-fat cooking methods such as microwaving, grilling, broiling, steaming, baking, and stewing.

DAILY GUIDELINES FOR FAT INTAKE

Intake in calories (kilojoules)	Total fat in grams	Saturated fat in grams
1500 (6270)	57	15
1800 (7524)	68	18
2000 (8360)	70	23
2500 (10450)	95	32

COOKING THE OIL-WATER SPRAY WAY

You can reduce the fat in cooking by using an oil-water spray, which delivers far less oil than commercial oil sprays. Fill a small plastic spray bottle with seven-eighths water and one-eighth oil of your choice.

Use your oil–water spray when cooking under the broiler, in a grill pan, in a skillet, or in roasting pans before adding foods. Alternatively, actually spray the food for broiling, grilling, frying, and roasting to give the lightest possible coating of oil. So don't brush—spray!

7 Choose Lean Meat, Poultry, Eggs, Beans, Nuts, Soy, and Low-fat Dairy Foods

Eat a variety of protein foods—choose a different one each day. Legumes are good for your heart: peas, beans (including baked, kidney, soy, and lima beans), lentils, and chickpeas are great sources of soluble fiber, which can help lower cholesterol. Soy protein also has a similar benefit. Nuts protect you from heart disease and you can eat up to four eggs a week.

8 Avoid Too Much Salt

Three-quarters of our salt intake now comes from salt added to processed food. So choose fresh foods rather than processed wherever possible, for example fresh meat and fish, fruit, and vegetables.

BELOW: Salt increases blood pressure so should definitely be kept out of any foods that are dedicated to a healthy heart diet.

♥ Avoid obviously salty foods—salted nuts, chips, canned fish, ham, bacon, sausages, corned beef, canned foods, dried soups, store-bought pies, cheeses, and salad dressings.

♥ The easiest way to cut your salt intake is not to add it to food, either while cooking or at the table. Kosher salt and sea salts are also sodium chloride and should be avoided. Replace the taste with fresh and dried herbs as well as other flavorings such as lemon juice, garlic, ginger, and vinegars.

♥ Remember some foods that do not appear to be salty, such as bread and some cereals, may contain large quantities of salt. Again, check the label!

9 Enjoy Alcohol With Your Food but be Sensible

If you like alcohol, then enjoy a glass or two each day with your meal. It is the pattern of drinking and the amount and strength of what you consume that are the important factors rather than the type of drink. Avoid binge drinking and keep to safe levels of alcohol, with some alcohol-free days.

10 Try to Walk for Half an Hour Most Days

Eating for a healthy heart is part of a whole healthy lifestyle, which involves not smoking and being physically active. Brisk walking, cycling, or climbing the stairs will benefit your heart. This will help you get fitter, control your weight, and improve your HDL cholesterol. So keep moving!

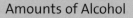

Amounts of Alcohol

1 alcoholic beverage =

1 small beer, lager, or cider
   (12 fl oz)
1 small glass of red or
   white wine
   (5 fl oz)
1 shot of spirits
   (1.5 fl oz)
1 small glass of fortified wine,
   e.g. sherry, vermouth
   (3 fl oz)

LEFT: Don't worry if you do not enjoy exercise—try and find something active that you know you will be able to include in your day-to-day life. Even "just walking" is perfectly suitable.

A Healthy Heart Diet

	Best Choice	In Moderation	Best Avoided
Cereals & Starchy Foods	Bread, chapatis, breakfast cereals, oats, porridge, rice, pasta, popcorn (without butter), all other cereals	Nan bread	Pappadams (fried), waffles, croissants, Danish pastries, fried rice, noodles in cartons
Potatoes	Boiled, mashed, baked, instant (without fat)	Oven french fries, roast potatoes cooked in best-choice oil, fat-free potato chips	French fries, potato croquettes, all other potato chips
Vegetables & Fruit	A wide variety of vegetables, fruit, salads, legumes—raw (except for legumes), baked, boiled, steamed, and all fresh, frozen, dried, canned	Stir-fried vegetables in best-choice oils, coleslaw in homemade dressing, canned fruit in syrup	Ready-made coleslaw; vegetables in batter
Fish	White fish: cod, haddock, flounder, lemon sole, whiting; oily fish: mackerel, herring, salmon, tuna, trout; canned fish in water or tomato sauce: tuna, pilchards, sardines; shellfish: oysters, mussels, clams, whelks, winkles, scallops; squid	Canned fish in oil (drain or rinse off excess oil); fish in bread crumbs; shellfish: shrimp, prawns, lobster, crab	Fried fish in batter: scampi, whitebait; roe, fish pâté, taramasalata
Meat	Well-trimmed broiled steak, chicken and turkey (with skin removed), venison, rabbit	Lean lamb, beef, pork; lean ground beef; broiled lean burgers; lean ham, Canadian bacon and lean bacon; liver and kidney; low-fat sausage	Fatty meats, crackling and skin; duck, sausages, bulk sausage, luncheon meat, corned beef, pâté, Scotch eggs, and meat pies,
Vegetarian Choices	Tofu, soy protein, legumes, chestnuts	All fresh nuts	Check fat content of vegetarian ready-made dishes

	Best Choice	In Moderation	Best Avoided
Eggs & Dairy	Egg white, skim milk, low-fat yogurt, very low-fat cheese: cottage cheese, fat-free fromage frais	Lowfat, soy, goat's, sheep's milk and their products; Greek yogurt, fromage frais, crème fraîche, evaporated milk; cheese: reduced-fat hard cheese, Edam, brie, camembert, feta, ricotta, mozzarella, cheese spread	Whole eggs (no more than four a week); whole milk, condensed milk, cream; cheese: cheddar, Gouda, Gruyère, Roquefort, Stilton, cream cheese
Oils	Olive oil, rapeseed (canola) oil	Sunflower, corn, safflower, peanut and sesame seed oils	Lard, suet, ghee, and some vegetable oils, particularly palm and coconut oil
Spreads	Plant sterol or stanol spreads, low-fat spreads	Olive, rapeseed (canola), sunflower and soy oil spreads	Butter, hard margarines
Whole Meals	Pasta with vegetable sauce, paella, kedgeree, kebabs skewered with best-choice ingredients, homemade soups	Homemade pizza, shepherd's pie, chili con carne, fish pie, casseroles	Fish and chips, lasagne, pasta in cream sauce, pies, quiches, samosas, cream soups
Cakes & Cookies	Homemade using best-choice ingredients; crispbreads, crumpets, rice cakes, matzos, breadsticks	Scones, fatless sponge cake; plain and semi-sweet cookies, crackers	Cakes: ready-made, rich, sponge cake, fresh cream; doughnuts, pastries, chocolate cookies
Other Desserts	Homemade using best-choice ingredients; meringue, lowfat milk puddings, jello, sherbet	Frozen yogurt, ice cream, milk puddings, crumbles	Cheesecake, pastry, suet puddings
Flavorings, Sauces, Jams, & Candies	Pepper, herbs, spices, lemon juice, vinegar, garlic, tomato paste, mustard; homemade salad dressings and sauces made with best-choice ingredients; jam, marmalade, honey	Tomato ketchup, brown sauce, Worcestershire sauce, pickles, bouillon cubes, gravy granules, reduced-calorie mayonnaise and salad dressing; hummus, peanut butter; mints, and hard candies	Salt, salad dressing, mayonnaise, cream sauces, ready-made sauces, chocolate spread, chocolates, toffees, fudge

Check the Label!

Label Checklist
Choose foods making general claims such as:
- ❤ Healthy eating
- ❤ Diet, reduced-calorie, or low-calorie
- ❤ Reduced-fat, low-fat, or virtually fat-free
- ❤ Sugar-free
- ❤ Low-salt or reduced-salt

But beware:
- ❤ Some low-fat products may be full of sugar and therefore higher in calories than the standard product
- ❤ Cholesterol-free foods may still have plenty of fat and calories
- ❤ Sugar-free doesn't mean low-calorie or low-fat; such foods may be high in both

To help you make the right choices when buying food, always check the label. A lot of food eaten today is processed and it is sometimes difficult to know exactly what you are eating. Processed food has to have a label listing the main ingredients. The ingredients are always listed in order of weight, so that the main ingredient is first on the list.

Since you won't have time while shopping to read everything, here are some details that you can check at a glance.

Nutrition Facts
Check the calories, fat, and saturated fat and check the size of the serving. Compare similar products and choose the brand with the lowest figures. The fat content is probably the most useful piece of information.

UNDERSTANDING THE FAT CONTENT
The table opposite will help you to understand the details of fat content on food labels. In the example given here, the entire pizza contains nearly 20 g of fat and therefore one-third to one-fifth of the recommended fat for a day.

As a general rule, reject any food that has more than 5 g fat per 3½ oz, especially when most of the fat is in the form of saturates. Choose oils and spreads that are rich in monounsaturates, and remember to avoid hydrogenated vegetable oil (trans fats).

CHECKING PORTION SIZES
Look at the amount per serving. Work out from the 'Ready reckoner' opposite whether there is a little or a lot of each nutrient in the food. Remember that the most important items to look for are calories, fat, and sodium (salt).

THE SALT CONTENT
Try to keep your daily sodium intake to below 2.5 g = 2500 mg sodium (6 g salt). In practice, this is hard to do since most of our daily intake comes from processed foods.

Reading Labels

The example below shows you how to read a food label and get the information you need. Use it in conjunction with the nutritional information opposite and the Ready Reckoner below to make sure you know exactly what you are eating.

protein • measured in grams (g)

• most people eat more than enough protein so special guidelines aren't needed

carbohydrate • measured in grams (g)

• this includes sugars and starches

• it includes natural and added sugars

• "of which sugars" is the amount of carbohydrate that comes from sugar

fiber • measured in grams (g)

• fiber is found in vegetables, fruit, beans, and pulses

• the Daily Reference Value (DRV) is 25 g for adults

sodium • measured in grams (g)

the Daily Reference Value (DRV) is 2.4 g for adults

energy • measured in calories (kcal)

• the amount of energy that a food gives you

• the Daily Reference Value (DRV) is 2500 calories for men and 2000 calories for women

fat • measured in grams (g)

• the total amount of fat in the food

• includes saturates, polyunsaturates, and monounsaturates

• eat less of all types especially saturates

• the Daily Reference Value (DRV) is 80 g for men and 65 g for women

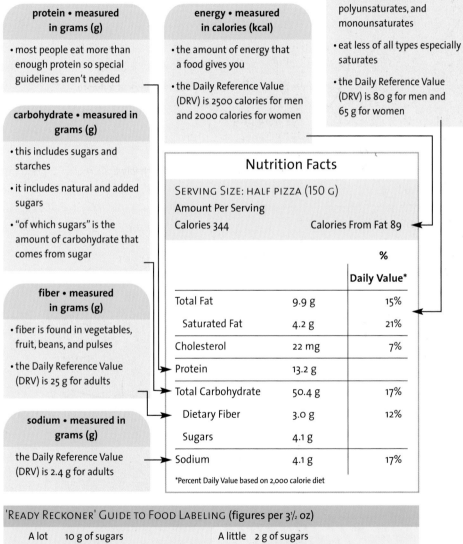

Nutrition Facts

SERVING SIZE: HALF PIZZA (150 G)

Amount Per Serving

Calories 344   Calories From Fat 89

		% Daily Value*
Total Fat	9.9 g	15%
Saturated Fat	4.2 g	21%
Cholesterol	22 mg	7%
Protein	13.2 g	
Total Carbohydrate	50.4 g	17%
Dietary Fiber	3.0 g	12%
Sugars	4.1 g	
Sodium	4.1 g	17%

*Percent Daily Value based on 2,000 calorie diet

'READY RECKONER' GUIDE TO FOOD LABELING (figures per 3½ oz)

A lot		A little	
	10 g of sugars		2 g of sugars
	20 g of fat		3 g of fat
	5 g saturated fat		1 g of saturated fat
	3 g of fiber		0.5 g of fiber
	500 mg sodium		100 mg of sodium

Source: The British Heart Foundation

The Recipes

breakfasts

walnut & banana sunrise smoothie

Preparation time: 10 minutes   **(V)**   **Serves 2**

NUTRITIONAL FACTS   ● calories – 300 (1254 kJ)   ● Fat – 10 g, of which less than 1 g saturated   ● Sodium – 110 mg

1 Place all the ingredients in a food processor or blender and blend until smooth and frothy. Pour into 2 glasses.

OR YOU COULD TRY...
Your own mixture of delicious fresh fruits, prepare as necessary, then whiz them up with nothing more than a handful of crushed ice. Try a mixture of the following:
1 banana, 2 handfuls fresh or frozen blackberries, 1 handful chopped fresh pineapple, $^2/_3$ cup plain yogurt, $^2/_3$ cup skim milk; or
2 handfuls fresh strawberries, 1 handful raspberries, $^2/_3$ cup strawberry soy yogurt, $^2/_3$ cup soy milk

1 orange, segmented
1 banana
$^2/_3$ **cup skim milk**
$^2/_3$ **cup plain yogurt**
$^1/_4$ **cup walnuts**
1 **tablespoon honey**

NUTRITIONAL TIPS
Smoothies are a great way to increase your intake of soy protein. Use the recipe above with soy milk and a soy yogurt to give you 10 g of soy protein. There are 5 g of soy protein in each $^2/_3$ cup soy milk and each $^2/_3$ cup soy yogurt.

light 'n' low crêpes

1 Sift the flour into a bowl. If using whole-wheat flour, also add the bran left in the sifter to the flour in the bowl.

2 Beat the egg, milk, and teaspoon of oil together, then slowly add to the flour. Stir the mixture until a smooth batter forms.

3 Let stand for about 20 minutes, then stir again.

4 Heat a little oil in a nonstick skillet, or spray with an oil-water spray. When the oil is hot, add 2 tablespoons of the crêpe batter and shake the pan so that it spreads.

5 Cook the crêpe for 2 minutes until the underside is lightly browned, then flip or turn over and cook the other side for a minute or so.

6 Keep the crêpes warm in the oven while you cook the rest—you can stack one on top of the other as they are cooked. The batter should make 8 crêpes in all. Serve with your chosen topping.

1 cup brown or whole-wheat flour
1 egg
1¼ cups skim milk (if using whole-wheat flour, you will need a little more)
1 teaspoon vegetable oil, plus a little extra for cooking, or use an oil-water spray (see page 14)

TOPPING IDEAS
chopped fresh fruit
chopped apple, raisins, and ground cinnamon
cottage cheese
low-fat cream cheese
fruit spread or preserve

*figures per serving – 2 crêpes, without topping

yogurt cups

Preparation time: less than 5 minutes   (V)   **Serves 1**

NUTRITIONAL FACTS*   ○ calories – 84 (353 kJ)   ○ Fat – 2 g, of which less than 1 g saturated   ○ Sodium – 125 mg

1 Add one or more of the flavorings to the yogurt and stir to mix.

OR YOU COULD TRY...
Having fruit with your breakfast to start the day well. A one-portion "fistful" of fruit contains less than 1 g of fat and no more than 100 calories. So choose from these two tropical fruit combinations (2 servings), preparing the fruit as necessary and mixing with the fresh fruit juice:
1 mango, 2 pineapple slices, 1 kiwifruit, 1 cup pineapple juice; or 4 passion fruit, 2 slices of melon, 1 nectarine, 1 cup passion fruit juice or tropical fruit juice.

²/₃ cup plain yogurt or soy yogurt

FLAVORING IDEAS
½ cup rolled oats
3 tablespoons unsweetened breakfast cereal
1 tablespoon pine nuts, sunflower seeds, or pumpkin seeds
1 tablespoon slivered almonds
1 tablespoon raisins or golden raisins
1 piece fresh fruit, such as a chopped apple or sliced banana
1 chopped fresh apricot or fig
1 small can peaches, pears, or pineapple (in natural juice with no added sugar), drained and chopped
1 stewed or pureed apple with a sprinkling of ground cinnamon
⅓ cup chopped dried fruit

*figures per ⅓ cup of plain yogurt

creamy oatmeal with summer berries

Preparation time: 5 minutes

Cooking time: 10–20 minutes

(V)   **Serves 2**

NUTRITIONAL FACTS   ○ calories – 280 (1176 kJ)   ○ Fat – 6 g of fat, of which less than 1 g saturated   ○ Sodium – 60 mg

1 Place the water and oats in a saucepan and bring to a boil. Simmer for 10–20 minutes, stirring occasionally.

2 Add the skim milk, stir, and simmer for a few more minutes.

3 Serve with your chosen berries.

OR YOU COULD TRY...

Sweetening your oatmeal with these other fruity combinations:

○ blueberries, loganberries, black currants, or red currants
○ raisins and golden raisins
○ apricots and figs
○ bananas and walnuts
○ prunes and a little honey

2½ cups water
1¼ cups rolled oats
⅔ cup skim milk
1 handful fresh, frozen and thawed, canned, or cooked berries, such as raspberries, strawberries, blackberries, or cranberries

NUTRITIONAL TIPS

Oats provide one of the richest sources of the dietary soluble fiber beta-glucan. The recommended intake for a cholesterol-lowering effect is 3 g of beta-glucan per day, which will reduce your total cholesterol by 6 mg/dl (0.2 mmol/l). This bowl of oatmeal would reduce your cholesterol by 4 mg/dl (0.1 mmol/l).

pumpkin seed & apricot muesli

Preparation time: 10 minutes

(V)

Serves 2

NUTRITIONAL FACTS   ● calories – 340 (1428 kJ)   ● Fat – 12 g, of which 1 g saturated fat   ● Sodium – 65 mg

1 Place the oats, raisins, seeds, almonds, and apricots in a bowl with the fruit juice or water.

2 Add the grated apple and stir to mix.

3 Top with skim milk, soy milk, plain yogurt, or soy yogurt.

OR YOU COULD TRY...
A softer texture, by soaking the oats and raisins with the fruit juice or water overnight.

½ cup rolled jumbo oats
1 tablespoon raisins
1 tablespoon pumpkin or
    sunflower seeds
1 tablespoon chopped almonds
2½ tablespoons ready-to-eat
    dried apricots, chopped
2 tablespoons fruit juice, such as
    apple or orange juice, or
    water
2 small eating apples, peeled
    and grated
3 tablespoons skim milk,
    soy milk, plain yogurt, or
    soy yogurt

NUTRITIONAL TIPS
Almonds and other nuts may help to lower your risk of heart disease. They are high in cardio-protective nutrients such as vitamin E, folate, magnesium, copper, and arginine. Almonds are the richest nut source of vitamin E, one of the antioxidants believed to play a role in reducing the risk of heart disease by preventing the oxidation of LDL cholesterol.

smoked mackerel and chive pâté

Preparation time: 10 minutes

Serves 8

NUTRITIONAL FACTS   ○ calories – 94 (395 kJ)   ○ Fat – 7 g, of which 1 g is saturated   ○ Sodium – 183 mg

1 Place the mackerel and cream cheese in a bowl and mash together well.

2 Add the remaining ingredients and mix well. Alternatively, mix all the ingredients together in a food processor or blender.

3 Spoon the mixture into 8 small individual serving dishes or 1 large serving dish or mold. Cover and refrigerate for at least 2 hours, or up to 4 hours. Serve the pâté chilled with Vegetable Sticks (see page 30) and whole-wheat toast, if you like.

OR YOU COULD TRY...
Using other omega-3-rich fish instead of mackerel in this recipe, such as canned (in water or brine), drained pilchards, salmon, or tuna.

7 oz smoked mackerel, skinned, boned, and flaked
½ cup low-fat cream cheese
1 bunch of chives, chopped
1 tablespoon fat-free vinaigrette
1 tablespoon lemon juice

NUTRITIONAL TIPS
Of all the oily fish which are readily available, mackerel is the richest source of omega-3 fatty acids, so enjoy it in all its many forms—fresh, canned, or smoked. It is also one of the least expensive oily fish.

tahini hummus

Preparation time: 10 minutes

(V)

Serves 6

NUTRITIONAL FACTS   ○ calories – 88 (370 kJ)   ○ Fat – 5 g, of which 0.6 g saturates   ○ Sodium – 93 mg

1 Place the chickpeas, tahini, garlic, lemon juice, and cumin in a food processor or blender. Puree until well blended, adding a little water or vegetable stock if you prefer a thinner consistency. Taste and add more garlic, lemon juice, or cumin to your liking.

2 Transfer the hummus to a serving bowl. Sprinkle with paprika or chopped parsley. Serve with Vegetable Sticks (see page 30) and Pita Bread Crisps (see below) or Turkish bread. Or use as an alternative to spread on bread.

SERVE WITH...
Pita bread crisps: cut a pita bread, either whole-wheat or white, into quarters or eighths. Split and separate each piece into two. Spread the pieces in a single layer on a nonstick baking sheet. Bake in a preheated 300°F oven for 10–15 minutes, until the pieces of bread are dried out and crisp.

2 cups canned chickpeas, rinsed and drained
2 tablespoons tahini (sesame seed paste)
3 garlic cloves, chopped
½ cup lemon juice
pinch of ground cumin
Vegetable Stock (see page 122) or water (optional)
paprika or chopped parsley, for garnishing

red pepper & scallion dip with vegetable sticks

Preparation time: 10 minutes

Cooking time: 30–40 minutes

V

Serves 4

NUTRITIONAL FACTS * ○ calories – 60 (252 kJ) ○ Fat – 1 g of fat, of which less than 0.5 g saturated ○ Sodium – 2 mg

1 Slightly flatten the pepper quarters and place on a baking sheet. Wrap the garlic in foil and place on the sheet. Roast in a preheated 425°F oven for 30–40 minutes until the pepper is slightly charred and the garlic is soft.

2 When cool enough to handle, remove the skin from the pepper and discard. Transfer the flesh to a bowl.

3 Squeeze the roasted garlic flesh from the cloves into the bowl.

4 Using a fork, roughly mash the pepper and garlic together. Stir in the soy yogurt and scallions. Season to taste with pepper. Serve with the vegetable sticks.

1 large red bell pepper, cut into
    quarters, cored, and seeded
2 garlic cloves, unpeeled
1 cup soy yogurt
2 scallions, finely chopped
freshly ground black pepper
selection of raw vegetables,
    such as carrots, cucumber, bell
    peppers, fennel, tomatoes,
    baby corn, snow peas, celery,
    and zucchini, cut into sticks,
    for serving

* figures for the dip only

NUTRITIONAL TIPS
This soy dip will provide you with 2 g soy protein. Research has shown that a daily intake of 25 g soy protein per day can significantly reduce total cholesterol as well as LDL cholesterol (the "bad guy") as part of a healthy diet.

spicy lentil & tomato soup

Preparation time: 20 minutes   **V**   **Serves 4**

Cooking time: 40–50 minutes

NUTRITIONAL FACTS   ○ calories – 288 (1210 kJ)   ○ Fat – 2 g, of which less than 1 g saturated   ○ Sodium – 117 mg

1 Heat the oil in a large pot, add the onion, garlic, and chili (if using), and fry gently for 4–5 minutes until soft.

2 Add the lentils, bay leaf, celery, carrots, leek, and stock. Cover and bring to a boil, then reduce the heat and simmer for 30–40 minutes until the lentils are soft. Remove the bay leaf.

3 Stir in the tomatoes, tomato paste, turmeric, ginger, cilantro, and pepper to taste. Let cool a little, then transfer to a food processor or blender. Puree until smooth, adding more stock or water if necessary.

4 Reheat gently, then serve with a swirl of yogurt and some crusty whole-wheat bread, if you like.

1 tablespoon vegetable oil
1 large onion, finely chopped
2 garlic cloves, finely chopped
1 small green chili, seeded and
   finely chopped (optional)
1⅓ cups red lentils, washed
   and drained
1 bay leaf
3 celery sticks, thinly sliced
3 carrots, thinly sliced
1 leek, thinly sliced
6 cups Vegetable Stock
   (see page 122)
13 oz canned chopped tomatoes
2 tablespoons tomato paste
½ teaspoon ground turmeric
½ teaspoon ground ginger
1 tablespoon chopped fresh
   cilantro
freshly ground black pepper
plain yogurt, for garnishing

NUTRITIONAL TIPS

All legumes—beans, peas, and lentils—are high in soluble fiber, which is good for cholesterol reduction. They also make a soup satisfying, and this lentil soup is particularly filling!

sweet potato & butternut squash soup

Preparation time: 20 minutes   **V**   **Serves 4**
Cooking time: 30 minutes
NUTRITIONAL FACTS   ○ calories – 260 (1092 kJ)   ○ Fat – 6 g, of which less than 1 g saturated   ○ Sodium – 206 mg

1 Heat the oil in a large pot and add the onion and garlic. Cover and cook very gently for 10 minutes, without coloring.

2 Add the spices, ginger, chili, lime zest, and honey, and stir for 30 seconds, then add the sweet potato, squash, half the lime juice, and the stock.

3 Cover and bring to a boil. Reduce the heat and simmer for about 10 minutes, until the vegetables are almost tender. Stir in the chickpeas. Check the seasoning and add pepper to taste. Simmer for another 10 minutes, then add the remaining lime juice to taste.

4 Let cool slightly, then puree in a food processor or blender until very smooth, adding more stock if necessary to achieve the desired consistency. Reheat gently and stir in the fresh cilantro just before serving.

1 tablespoon vegetable oil
1 onion, finely chopped
2 garlic cloves, finely chopped
1 teaspoon cumin seeds
1 teaspoon ground coriander
$\frac{1}{2}$ inch piece of fresh ginger
    root, peeled and finely grated
1 green chili, seeded and finely
    chopped
finely grated zest and juice of
    1 lime, set aside seperately
1 teaspoon honey
12 oz sweet potatoes, peeled
    and cut into small chunks
    (about 2$\frac{1}{2}$–3 cups)
12 oz butternut squash, peeled
    and cut into small chunks
    (about 3–3$\frac{1}{4}$ cups)
5 cups Vegetable Stock
    (see page 122)
2 cups canned chickpeas, rinsed
    and drained
handful of fresh cilantro
    leaves, chopped

fennel & white bean soup

Preparation time: 15 minutes
Cooking time: 30 minutes

(V)   **Serves 4**

NUTRITIONAL FACTS   ○ calories – 155 (657 kJ)   ○ Fat – 1 g, of which less than 1 g saturated   ○ Sodium – 550 mg

1 Place 1 cup of the stock in a large pot. Add the fennel, onion, zucchini, carrot, and garlic. Cover and bring to a boil. Continue boiling for 5 minutes, then remove the lid, reduce the heat, and simmer gently for about 20 minutes until the vegetables are tender.

2 Stir in the tomatoes, beans, and sage. Season to taste with pepper and pour in the remaining stock. Simmer for five minutes, then let the soup cool slightly.

3 Transfer 1 cup of the soup to a food processor or blender and puree until smooth. Return the blended portion to the pot, stir, and heat through gently.

$3^3/_4$ cups Vegetable Stock
(see page 122)
2 fennel bulbs, trimmed and
chopped
1 onion, chopped
1 zucchini, chopped
1 carrot, chopped
2 garlic cloves, finely sliced
6 tomatoes, finely chopped, or
13 oz canned tomatoes
26 oz canned lima beans, rinsed
and drained
2 tablespoons chopped
fresh sage
freshly ground black pepper

NUTRITIONAL TIPS
When buying canned vegetables, choose the "no added salt" varieties. If these are not available, rinse and drain vegetables such as beans and corn. This removes some, but not all, of the salt.

speedy mediterranean pasta

Preparation time: 10 minutes   V   **Serves 4**
Cooking time: 20 minutes
NUTRITIONAL FACTS   ● calories – 305 (1281 kJ)   ● Fat – 3 g, of which less than 1 g saturated fat   ● Sodium – 54 mg

1 Place all the ingredients, except the pasta and Parmesan, in a saucepan and simmer, uncovered, for 15 minutes.

2 Meanwhile, cook the pasta according to the package instructions until it is just tender.

3 Let the sauce cool a little, then transfer to a food processor or blender. Blend until smooth.

4 Drain the pasta, return to the pan, and toss with the sauce. Sprinkle with Parmesan, if you like, and serve with a green salad and French bread.

OR YOU COULD TRY...
Adding some of the following to the sauce to vary the flavor:
● Freshly steamed vegetables
● Canned beans, rinsed and drained
● Tuna, rinsed and drained
● Pitted olives
● A handful of walnuts

13 oz canned chopped tomatoes
1 onion, chopped
1 garlic clove, crushed
2 tablespoons chopped
    fresh basil
1 teaspoon dried rosemary
½ cup red wine (optional)
12 oz dried pasta
Parmesan cheese, for serving
    (optional)

crispy potato skins

Preparation time: 10 minutes   V   **Serves 2**
Cooking time: 1 hour 50 minutes
NUTRITIONAL FACTS   ● calories – 115 (483 kJ)   ● Fat – less than 1 g, of which negligible saturated   ● Sodium – 10 mg

1 Scrub the potatoes and place in a preheated 425°F oven for 1¼ hours until tender. Alternatively prick the potatoes and place on paper towels in the microwave and cook on maximum (100%) for 6 minutes, turn over, and cook for 7 minutes more, or follow the instructions in your microwave cookbook.

2 Cut the potatoes in half, scoop out the insides, leaving a shell about ¼ inch thick. (Save the scooped-out potato for another use, such as for a root veg mash or in a soup.) Cut each of the shells in half lengthways.

3 Spray a nonstick baking sheet with oil-water spray. Place the potato quarters, skin side down, on the sheet and spray lightly with the oil-water spray. Bake in a preheated 400°F oven for 25–35 minutes until golden brown and very crisp. Serve immediately.

OR YOU COULD TRY...
Them on their own with just a shower of black pepper and a squeeze of fresh lemon juice, with dips such as Tahini Hummus (see page 45) or Red Pepper and Scallion Dip (see page 46). Alternatively, they can also be served as a vegetable accompaniment to meat, poultry, or fish dishes when you want a potato dish with a crisp texture.

2 large baking potatoes
oil-water spray (see page 14)

NUTRITIONAL TIPS
By using the oil-water spray, these potato skins become a really low-fat snack compared to the conventional version which is usually topped with crispy bacon and cheese, and smothered in sour cream.

garlic, pea, & parmesan crostini

Preparation time: 25 minutes
Cooking time: 55 minutes

V

Serves 8

NUTRITIONAL FACTS   ○ calories – 200 (840 kJ)   ○ Fat – 12 g, of which 2 g saturated   ○ Sodium – 228 mg

1 Roast the garlic following the method for Garlic Mash (see page 72).

2 Meanwhile, to make the crostini, cut the loaf into 40 slices about ¼–½ inch thick. Using an oil-water spray or pastry brush, lightly coat each side of the bread slices with oil.

3 Place the bread slices on a rack and bake in a preheated 400°F oven for about 5–10 minutes, turning the bread over as it turns pale gold. Remove and let cool.

4 Cook the peas in boiling water until tender. Drain and puree in a food processor or blender, or mash in a bowl with a fork. Separate the garlic cloves, squeeze out the roasted garlic flesh, and add to the peas with the spread and Parmesan. Blend or mash to a creamy puree. Let cool before spreading onto the crostini. Garnish with parsley or mint, if you like.

1 head of garlic
1 French baguette
olive oil-water spray (see page 14) or a little olive oil
1²/₃ cups frozen peas
1 tablespoon unsaturated spread
2 tablespoons freshly grated Parmesan cheese
1 tablespoon chopped fresh mint
parsley for garnishing

OTHER CROSTINI TOPPINGS
Reduced-fat cream cheese and shrimp
Red or green pesto sauce
Green olive paste
Smoked Mackerel and Chive Pâté (see page 28)
Goat's cheese
Tahini Hummus (see page 29)

NUTRITIONAL TIPS
Crostini, made with olive oil, follows the beneficial Mediterranean diet rule for an appetizer or snack. Olive oil is a rich source of monounsaturates and vitamin E. Add lots of vegetables to the toppings for extra antioxidant nutrients.

mediterranean vegetable & walnut salad

Preparation time: 30 minutes   **V**   **Serves 6**

NUTRITIONAL FACTS   ● calories – 300 (1260 kJ)   ● Fat – 13 g, of which 1 g saturated   ● Sodium – 550 mg

1 Heat the walnuts in a dry pan over medium heat for 1–2 minutes until slightly toasted. Set aside.

2 Whisk together the olive vinaigrette and olives in a small bowl.

3 Mix together the chickpeas, pepper, carrot, and onion in a medium bowl. Toss with 3 tablespoons of the vinaigrette.

4 Toss the spinach and other salad greens with the remaining vinaigrette. Transfer to a large serving bowl, top with the vegetable mixture, and sprinkle with the toasted walnuts.

³/₄ cup chopped walnuts

¹/₃ cup Olive Vinaigrette (see page 123)

1 tablespoon chopped pitted olives

13 oz canned chickpeas, drained

1 red bell pepper, cored, seeded, and thinly sliced

1 large carrot, cut into matchsticks

1 small red onion, thinly sliced

4 handfuls of baby spinach

4 handfuls of salad greens

NUTRITIONAL TIPS
Walnuts are one of the richest plant sources of omega-3 fatty acids available. A handful of walnuts provides as much omega-3 as a 3-oz portion of salmon. Walnut oil is also rich in omega-3.

oriental-style coleslaw

Preparation time: 20 minutes   (V)   **Serves 6**

NUTRITIONAL FACTS   O calories – 160 (672 kJ)   O Fat – 10 g, of which 1 g saturated   O Sodium – 35 mg

1 Place all the salad ingredients in a large serving bowl and toss them well to combine.

2 For the dressing, heat the sesame seeds in a small, dry saucepan over medium heat, shaking the pan frequently for 2–3 minutes until toasted.

3 Stir in the remaining dressing ingredients. Remove the pan from the heat, immediately pour the dressing over the salad. Toss to combine.

OR YOU COULD TRY...

Varying the coleslaw recipe above by substituting or adding one or more of the following ingredients: green cabbage, fennel, celery, onions, apples, oranges, sunflower seeds, pumpkin seeds, dried fruit such as raisins, golden raisins, and ready-to-eat apricots, walnuts, pine nuts, garlic, fresh herbs.

1 daikon radish, cut into long, thin strips

1 large carrot, cut into long, thin strips

½ Chinese cabbage, shredded

¼ red cabbage, shredded

2 scallions, cut into long, thin strips

18 snow peas, cut lengthways into thin strips

a large handful spinach, shredded

2 fresh or 4 dried figs, cut lengthways into quarters

1 cup slivered almonds

DRESSING

2 tablespoons sesame seeds

1 tablespoon grated fresh ginger root

1 teaspoon sugar

3 tablespoons sherry vinegar or rice wine vinegar

2 teaspoons peanut oil

2 teaspoons reduced-salt soy sauce

a few drops of sesame oil (optional)

baked beets, spinach, & orange salad

Preparation time: 20 minutes
Cooking time: 1–2 hours

(V)   **Serves 4**

NUTRITIONAL FACTS   ● calories – 125 (525 kJ)   ● Fat – 2 g, of which less than 1 g saturated   ● Sodium – 410 mg

1 To bake the beets, place the whole beets on a piece of foil large enough to enclose them loosely, scatter with the garlic and oregano. Season to taste with pepper and drizzle the oil and vinegar over them.

2 Gather up the foil loosely and fold over at the top to seal. Place on a baking sheet and bake in a preheated 400°F oven for 1–2 hours, depending upon the size of the beets, until tender.

3 Remove from the oven and let them cool before peeling and slicing them. Discard the garlic.

4 Place the spinach in a layer in the bottom of a large salad bowl followed by alternate layers of beet slices and orange segments.

5 Drizzle the dressing over them and season with pepper to taste. Garnish with oregano.

OR YOU COULD TRY...
The baked beets are also delicious served hot as a vegetable accompaniment to meat and fish, or roughly mashed to a puree, in which case the baked garlic can be added to the mash.

1 lb raw whole beets, preferably of even size
2 garlic cloves
handful of fresh oregano leaves
1 teaspoon olive oil
1 tablespoon balsamic vinegar
7 oz baby spinach
2 oranges, segmented
⅓ cup Olive Vinaigrette (see page 123)
freshly ground black pepper
chopped oregano, for garnishing

NUTRITIONAL TIPS
Beets are important for heart health as they contain a high amount of antioxidants, as indicated by their vibrant color. They also contain other beneficial vitamins and minerals including beta carotene, vitamins B6 and C, folic acid, manganese, calcium, magnesium, iron, potassium, and phosphorus—all important for heart health.

tabbouleh

Preparation time: 15 minutes, plus standing   (V)   **Serves 6**

NUTRITIONAL FACTS   ○ calories – 134 (563 kJ)   ○ Fat – 22 g, of which a less than 1 g saturated   ○ Sodium – 8 mg

1 Place the bulghur wheat in a bowl. Pour the boiling water over it to cover, and let stand for 45–60 minutes until the grains swell and soften.

2 Drain and press to remove excess moisture. Place in a salad bowl. Add the onion, tomatoes, cucumber, parsley, and mint. Toss to combine.

3 For the dressing, place the ingredients in a screw-top jar, replace the lid, and shake well to combine. Pour it over the salad and toss to coat. Cover and refrigerate until ready to use—within 2–3 days.

OR YOU COULD TRY...

Tabbouleh as an accompaniment for fish and meat dishes, such as Orange and Cider Poached Mackerel (see page 65) or Turkish Lamb and Potato Stew (see page 105). It is also tasty as a baked potato topping or as a filling for pita bread.

1 cup bulghur wheat
1¼ cups boiling water
1 red onion, finely chopped
3 tomatoes, diced
¼ cucumber, chopped
⅔ cup chopped parsley
⅓ cup chopped mint

DRESSING
⅓ cup plus 1 tablespoon
    lemon juice
2 teaspoons olive oil
freshly ground black pepper

three bean & tuna salad

Preparation time: 15 minutes   **Serves 6**
Cooking time: 5 minutes
NUTRITIONAL FACTS   O calories – 130 (546 kJ)   O Fat – 3 g, of which less than 1 g saturated   O Sodium – 560 mg

1 If using fresh or frozen green beans, lightly cook for 4–5 minutes in boiling water, or steam or microwave. Refresh under cold running water, then drain well.

2 Flake the tuna and place in a bowl with all the beans and the onion.

3 Mix together the dressing ingredients and pour the dressing over the bean and tuna salad.

4 Toss lightly and garnish with olives. Serve on a bed of salad greens.

6 oz green beans (15–18 beans), canned, fresh, or frozen
6$\frac{1}{4}$ oz canned tuna, rinsed and drained
1 cup canned lima beans, rinsed and drained
1 cup canned red kidney beans, rinsed and drained
1 onion, finely sliced
12 olives, for garnishing
salad greens, for serving

DRESSING
1 teaspoon Dijon mustard
2 tablespoons balsamic vinegar
1 tablespoon olive oil
1 tablespoon tomato paste
1 small garlic clove, crushed
2 tablespoons chopped parsley
pinch of dried basil or oregano
freshly ground black pepper

NUTRITIONAL TIPS
The many beans in this dish are abundant in cardio-protective nutrients. Combined with low-fat canned tuna, this salad is a healthy complement to any meal.

orange & almond couscous salad

Preparation time: 15 minutes, plus standing
Cooking time: 5 minutes

Ⓥ

Serves 6

NUTRITIONAL FACTS ● calories – 160 (672 kJ) ● Fat – 4 g, of which 0.3 g saturated ● Sodium – 6 mg

1 Place the apple juice in a saucepan and bring to a boil. Slowly stir in the couscous. Remove the pan from the heat. Cover and let stand for 10 minutes. Fluff up with a fork.

2 Add the pepper, herbs, and currants to the couscous. Toss to combine. Transfer to a serving bowl. Scatter with the orange segments and onion.

3 For the dressing, place the dressing ingredients in a small saucepan and heat gently to dissolve the honey—do not let it boil. Drizzle the dressing over the salad. Scatter with the almonds.

1 cup apple juice
1 cup couscous
½ red bell pepper, cored, seeded, and cut into squares
¼ cup chopped parsley
3 tablespoons chopped mint
3 tablespoons currants
2 oranges, segmented
1 red onion, sliced
⅓ cup slivered almonds

DRESSING
juice of 1 orange
juice of 1 lemon or lime
2 teaspoons olive or hazelnut oil
1 teaspoon honey

NUTRITIONAL TIPS
Almonds (see also the Nutritional Tip on page 26) contain the amino acid arginine (among other vital nutrients), which is thought to improve the health of artery linings and reduce the risk of heart disease.

caponata ratatouille

Preparation time: 20 minutes
Cooking time: 40 minutes
NUTRITIONAL FACTS   ○ calories – 90 (378 kJ)   ○ Fat – 4 g, of which 1 g saturated   ○ Sodium – 155 mg

V   **Serves 6**

1 Cut the eggplants and onions into ½-inch chunks and set aside in separate piles.

2 Heat the oil in a nonstick skillet until very hot, add the eggplant, and fry for about 15 minutes until very soft. Add a little boiling water to prevent sticking if necessary.

3 Meanwhile, place the onion and celery in a saucepan with a little water or wine. Cook for about 5 minutes, until tender but still firm.

4 Add the tomatoes, thyme, cayenne pepper, fried eggplant, and cooked onions and celery. Cook for 15 minutes, stirring occasionally.

5 Add the capers, olives, wine vinegar, sugar, and cocoa powder (if using), and cook for 2–3 minutes. Season with pepper and serve garnished with almonds and parsley. Serve hot or cold as a side dish, appetizer, or a main dish. Serve with polenta and hot crusty bread, if you like.

1½ lb eggplants
1 large Spanish onion
1 tablespoon olive oil
3 celery sticks, coarsely chopped
a little wine (optional)
2 large beefsteak tomatoes,
    skinned and seeded
1 teaspoon chopped fresh thyme
¼–½ teaspoon cayenne pepper
2 tablespoons capers
handful of pitted green olives
¼ cup wine vinegar
1 tablespoon sugar
1–2 tablespoons cocoa powder
    (optional)
freshly ground black pepper

FOR GARNISHING
toasted, chopped almonds
chopped parsley

NUTRITIONAL TIPS
Eggplants can absorb a lot of fat when fried and therefore it is important to measure the amount of olive oil and not be tempted to add any more. Instead of using oil, you can sauté vegetables in wine, water, or stock with tasty results.

spicy pinto & cranberry beans in tomato sauce

Preparation time: 10 minutes
Cooking time: 20 minutes

V

Serves 4

NUTRITIONAL FACTS   ⊙ calories – 170 (714 kJ)   ⊙ Fat – 1 g, of which less than 1 g saturated   ⊙ Sodium – 160 mg

1 Mix together the onions, garlic, chili, spices, and just over a cup of the stock in a skillet. Cover and boil for 5 minutes. Uncover and simmer briskly for about 5 minutes until the onions are tender and the liquid has almost gone.

2 Stir in the remaining stock, beans, and tomato puree. Simmer, partially covered, for about 10 minutes until thick.

3 Stir in the lime juice and herbs. Season to taste with pepper. This dish can be used as an alternative to refried beans as part of a Mexican meal. You can use any canned beans but the cranberry and pinto beans give a lovely pink color to this dish.

2 onions, chopped
4 garlic cloves, crushed
1 chili, seeded and chopped
1 tablespoon ground cumin
½ tablespoon ground coriander
1½ cups Vegetable Stock
 (see page 122)
1¼ cups canned pinto beans,
 rinsed and drained
1¼ cups canned cranberry beans,
 rinsed and drained
1¼ cups tomato puree
juice of 1 lime
2 tablespoons each chopped
 parsley, mint, and cilantro
freshly ground black pepper

NUTRITIONAL TIPS
While legume protein is valuable, it can be made more so by combining it with protein from cereal foods. This nutritional principle may not be familiar to you, but the practical examples certainly will be—lentil soup with bread, rice and beans, Indian dal with rice or chapatis, and spicy beans with tortillas.

indian-spiced mushroom & pea sauté

Preparation time: 10 minutes
Cooking time: 20 minutes

(V)　　　　　**Serves 4**

NUTRITIONAL FACTS　　● calories – 90 (378 kJ)　● Fat – 4 g, of which 0.5 g saturated　● Sodium – 15 mg

1 Heat the oil in a saucepan, add the onion, and fry gently for 2–3 minutes until it begins to soften. Add the cumin and mustard seeds and fry, stirring, for another 2 minutes.

2 Add the tomatoes, chili, mushrooms, and peas. Stir and cook for 2 minutes.

3 Add the chili powder and turmeric, mix well, then cook, uncovered, for another 5–7 minutes.

4 Add the pepper, garlic, and cilantro leaves and cook for 5 minutes until the mixture is quite dry. Garnish with the scallions or chives. Serve as a vegetable accompaniment to Tandoori Chicken (see page 104) or Kofta Curry (see page 106), if you like.

2 tablespoons vegetable oil

3½ tablespoons finely sliced onion

¼ teaspoon cumin seeds, crushed

¼ teaspoon mustard seeds

⅔ cup chopped tomatoes

1 green chili, seeded and finely chopped

14 oz button mushrooms (about 4–5 cups), halved (or quartered, if larger)

1¼ cups frozen peas

½ teaspoon chili powder

¼ teaspoon turmeric

1 red bell pepper, cored, seeded, and chopped

4 garlic cloves, crushed

2 tablespoons fresh cilantro leaves

chopped scallions or chives, for garnishing

spiced roast roots

Preparation time: 20 minutes
Cooking time: 40 minutes

(V)   **Serves 6**

NUTRITIONAL FACTS   ● calories – 100 (420 kJ)   ● Fat – 3 g, of which less than 1 g saturated   ● Sodium – 30 mg

1 Place all the vegetables and garlic in a large roasting pan. Sprinkle over them the crushed seeds and squeeze the ginger pulp over them to extract the juice. Season to taste with pepper and drizzle with the oil.

2 Roast in a preheated 400°F oven for 30 minutes, turning occasionally.

3 Pour the wine over them and return to the oven for another 10 minutes. Garnish with parsley. Serve as a side dish or as a main meal, with freshly baked bread toasted with a topping of reduced-fat cheese.

4 carrots, thickly sliced diagonally
8 oz rutabaga, cubed (about 1¼–1½ cups)
8 oz sweet potato, cubed (about 1¼–1½ cups)
1 onion, cut into 8 wedges
2 leeks, thickly sliced diagonally
6 garlic cloves
½ teaspoon mustard or cumin seeds, lightly crushed
½ teaspoon coriander seeds, lightly crushed
1 inch piece fresh ginger root, peeled and finely grated
1 tablespoon olive oil
½ cup dry white wine
freshly ground black pepper
1 tablespoon flat-leaf parsley, for garnishing

NUTRITIONAL TIPS
Garlic is thought to be good for your heart but not enough scientific trials have yet been carried out to confirm the benefits. It certainly contains a substance called allicin, which dilates the blood vessels and reduces blood clotting.

speedy vegetable stir-fry

Preparation time: 10 minutes

Cooking time: 10 minutes

NUTRITIONAL FACTS   ○ calories – 300 (1260 kJ)   ○ Fat – 12 g, of which 2 g saturated   ○ Sodium – 775 mg

(V)

Serves 6

1 Prepare the noodles according to the package instructions.

2 Meanwhile, heat the oil to a high heat in a wok or skillet. Add the baby corn, snow peas, and pepper, and stir-fry for 2 minutes. Then add the baby spinach or other leafy green vegetable, shallot, garlic, and ginger, and stir-fry for another 1–2 minutes.

3 Drain the noodles and add them to the pan. Stir-fry for 1 minute. Drizzle with sauce to taste before serving.

3 oz fresh rice ribbon noodles or fine egg noodles

handful each of baby corn, snow peas, baby spinach, or other leafy green vegetable

½ red bell pepper, cored, seeded, and cut into fine strips

1 shallot, finely chopped

1 garlic clove, chopped

1 inch piece fresh ginger root, peeled and grated

2 teaspoons Teriyaki Sauce (see page 124) or oyster sauce

2 teaspoons sesame oil

NUTRITIONAL TIPS

Stir-frying is a quick and healthy method of cooking. You should use only a small amount of oil and cook the food quickly to retain all the nutrients. The oil should be very hot, to seal the food and limit the absorption of fat. Do not be tempted to add extra oil when stir-frying to prevent the food from sticking. Remember that you can also stir-fry with water, wine, sherry, or stock.

thai-style angler fish & mushroom kebabs

Preparation time: 15 minutes, plus marinating
Cooking time: 10 minutes

Serves 4

NUTRITIONAL FACTS ● calories – 192 (806 kJ) ● Fat – 5 g, of which less than 1 g saturated ● Sodium – 34 mg

1 Combine the ingredients for the marinade in a large bowl. Cut the fish into large cubes and add to the marinade along with the onion, mushrooms, and zucchini. Cover and refrigerate for 1 hour for the flavors to blend.

2 Brush the rack of a broiler pan lightly with oil to prevent the kebabs from sticking. Thread 4 skewers with alternate chunks of fish, mushrooms, zucchini, and onion. Brush with a little oil and broil under a preheated hot broiler for about 10 minutes, turning at intervals. Garnish with watercress or flat-leaf parsley.

OR YOU COULD TRY...
Any firm white fish such as halibut, sea bass, swordfish, cod, or haddock, if you prefer.

1–1½ lb angler fish tails, skinned
1 onion, quartered, and layers separated
8 mushrooms
1 zucchini, cut into 8 pieces
vegetable oil, for brushing
watercress or flat-leaf parsley, for garnishing

MARINADE
grated zest and juice of 2 limes
1 garlic clove, finely chopped
2 tablespoons finely sliced fresh ginger root
2 fresh chilies, red or green or 1 of each, seeded and finely chopped
2 lemon grass stalks, finely chopped
handful of chopped fresh cilantro
½ cup red wine
2 tablespoons sesame oil
freshly ground black pepper

crab & cilantro cakes

Preparation time: 25–30 minutes

Cooking time: 10 minutes

Serves 6

NUTRITIONAL FACTS   ○ calories – 185 (777 kJ)   ○ Fat – 5 g, of which 1 g saturated   ○ Sodium – 509 mg

1 In a large bowl, mix together the crabmeat, mashed potatoes, cilantro, scallions, lemon zest and juice, and half the beaten egg to bind.

2 Form the mixture into 12 cakes about ½ inch thick. Coat the cakes with flour, then dip into the remaining egg and then the bread crumbs.

3 Heat the oil in a nonstick skillet and fry the cakes for about 10 minutes until golden, turning once or twice.

4 Drain on paper towels before serving. Serve with a sweet red chili sauce or Tomato Salsa (see page 125).

OR YOU COULD TRY...

Using canned tuna or salmon, or fresh fish, and adding peas or corn. Try making a vegetable version using peas, broccoli, and carrots instead of fish.

12 oz canned crabmeat, drained (about 1½ cups)
1 cup cold mashed potatoes
2 tablespoons chopped fresh cilantro
1 bunch of scallions, finely sliced
grated zest and juice of ½ lemon
2 eggs, beaten
flour, for coating
5 oz fresh white bread crumbs (about 2½–3 cups)
1 tablespoon oil

NUTRITIONAL TIPS

Canned crabmeat contains a moderate amount of omega-3 fatty acids (0.91 g omega-3 per 100 g). Canned fish is saltier than fresh fish (unless it is canned in water), so lower the salt content by putting the fish in a strainer or colander and rinsing it under cold running water. Drain thoroughly on paper towels.

parsley & garlic marinated sardines

Preparation time: 10 minutes
Cooking time: 5 minutes

Serves 6

NUTRITIONAL FACTS ○ calories – 180 (756 kJ) ○ Fat – 10 g, of which 2.5g saturated ○ Sodium – 112 mg

1 Place all the ingredients for the marinade in a small saucepan. Bring to a boil, then remove from the heat.

2 Place the sardines on a prepared barbecue or on a preheated hot grill pan or under a hot broiler. Cook for 1–2 minutes on each side until crisp and golden.

3 Place the sardines in a single layer in a shallow dish. Pour the dressing over the sardines and serve hot. Alternatively, cover and refrigerate for at least 1 hour before serving cold. Serve with Tabbouleh (see page 44) and a mixed green salad, if you like.

OR YOU COULD TRY...

Draining a can of sardines and pureeing it in a food processor with 1 crushed garlic clove, 1 tablespoon drained capers, 6 pitted black olives, some chopped parsley, and 1 tablespoon of wine vinegar or balsamic vinegar. Puree until blended. Spread on piping hot toast for a delicious snack or appetizer.

12 fresh sardines, cleaned, or use fillets if you prefer

MARINADE
2 oz chopped parsley (about 2 cups)
1 teaspoon freshly ground black pepper
1 garlic clove, crushed
finely grated zest and juice of 1 lemon
2 tablespoons white wine
1 tablespoon olive oil

NUTRITIONAL TIPS
A 3½-oz portion of fresh sardines contains 2.7 g of omega-3 fatty acids. This Mediterranean recipe is equally suitable for other types of fish that are high in omega-3 fatty acids (see page 12), such as mackerel and salmon.

french lentils with flaked salmon & dill weed

Preparation time: 30 minutes

Serves 4

Cooking time: 45 minutes

NUTRITIONAL FACTS ◐ calories – 450 (1890 kJ) ◐ Fat – 18 g, of which 3 g saturated ◐ Sodium – 70 mg

1 Place the salmon on a sheet of foil and spoon the wine over it. Gather up the foil and fold over at the top to seal. Place on a baking sheet and bake in a preheated 400°F oven for 15–20 minutes, until cooked. Let cool, then flake, cover, and chill.

2 Flatten the pepper halves slightly. Broil, skin side up, under a preheated hot broiler until charred. Enclose in a plastic bag for a few minutes. Remove from the bag, peel away the skin, and cut the flesh into 1-inch cubes, reserving any juices.

3 Place all the dressing ingredients, except the oil, in a food processor or blender and blend until smooth. While blending, drizzle in the oil until the mixture is thick.

4 Place the lentils in a large saucepan with plenty of water, bring to a boil, then simmer gently for about 15–20 minutes until cooked but still firm to the bite. Drain and place in a bowl with the pepper, dill weed, most of the scallions, and pepper to taste.

5 Stir the dressing into the hot lentils and let it infuse. To serve, top the lentils with the flaked salmon and gently mix the salmon through the lentils and dressing, squeeze a little lemon juice over it and scatter the remaining scallions on top.

1 lb salmon tail fillet

2 tablespoons dry white wine

4 red bell peppers, cut in half, cored, and seeded

scant cup French lentils, well rinsed

large handful of dill weed, chopped

1 bunch of scallions, finely sliced

lemon juice, for squeezing

freshly ground black pepper

DRESSING

2 garlic cloves

large handful of flat-leaf parsley, chopped

large handful of dill weed, chopped

1 teaspoon Dijon mustard

2 green chilies, seeded and chopped

juice of 2 large lemons

1 tablespoon extra virgin olive oil

chili & cilantro fish parcels

Preparation time: 15 minutes, plus marinating

Serves 1

Cooking time: 15 minutes

NUTRITIONAL FACTS   ● calories – 127 (533 kJ)   ● Fat – 1 g, of which 0.2g saturated   ● Sodium – 90 mg

1 Place the fish in a non-metallic dish and sprinkle with the lemon juice. Cover and let marinate in the refrigerator for 15–20 minutes.

2 Place the cilantro, garlic, and chili in a food processor or blender and blend until the mixture forms a paste. Add the sugar and yogurt and briefly blend to combine.

3 Place the fish on a sheet of foil. Coat the fish on both sides with the paste. Gather up the foil loosely and fold over at the top to seal. Return to the refrigerator for at least 1 hour.

4 Place the wrapped fish on a baking tray and bake in a preheated 400°F oven for about 15 minutes, until the fish is just cooked.

OR YOU COULD TRY...

Combining, for example, chicken, steak, or salmon with your favorite vegetables and herbs and baking in foil to provide a flavorful dish complete with its own homemade sauce.

4 oz cod, pollock, or haddock
    fillet
2 teaspoons lemon juice
1 tablespoon fresh cilantro
    leaves
1 garlic clove
1 green chili, seeded and
    chopped
¼ teaspoon sugar
2 teaspoons plain yogurt

NUTRITIONAL TIPS

Cod is a low-fat white fish, a good source of protein and a useful source of iron. It has only 0.3 g omega-3 fatty acids per 4-oz portion, but nevertheless will still make a contribution to your omega-3 intake. People who eat fish regularly are less likely to die of heart disease than those who rarely or never eat it.

tuna & mixed vegetable pasta casserole

Preparation time: 10 minutes

Cooking time: 30 minutes

NUTRITIONAL FACTS ● calories – 400 (1680 kJ) ● Fat – 6 g, of which 1 g saturated ● Sodium – 425 mg

1 Heat the oil in a nonstick skillet, add the onion, and fry for about 5 minutes until soft.

2 Meanwhile, cook the macaroni according to the package instructions, until just tender. Drain.

3 Mix the pasta with the onion, tuna, tomatoes, vegetables, cottage cheese, and fromage frais or yogurt. Pour into a greased casserole or ovenproof dish. Top with the bread crumbs.

4 Bake in a preheated 350°F oven for about 30 minutes, until golden on top. Serve with a mixed salad and Potato & Olive Bread (see page 70), if you like.

1 tablespoon vegetable oil

1 onion, chopped

2$\frac{1}{4}$ cups whole-wheat macaroni

7 oz canned tuna, well drained and flaked

13 oz canned tomatoes

1 cup cooked mixed frozen vegetables

$\frac{1}{2}$ cup cottage cheese with chives

2 tablespoons plain fromage frais or yogurt

3 oz whole-wheat bread crumbs (about 1$\frac{1}{2}$ cups)

NUTRITIONAL TIPS

Canned tuna contains fewer omega-3 fatty acids than fresh tuna and other canned forms of oily fish because much of the fat is lost when it is pre-cooked before canning. This does not happen to the more oil-rich salmon, mackerel, sardines, or pilchards. Nevertheless, canned tuna is a very useful low-fat and low-calorie fish, to keep in your cupboard.

grilled honey-glazed tuna with parsnip puree

Preparation time: 15 minutes

Cooking time: 15 minutes

Serves 4

NUTRITIONAL FACTS ● calories – 310 (1302 kJ) ● Fat – 10 g, of which 2 g saturated ● Sodium – 300 mg

1 Place the ingredients for the glaze in a small saucepan. Bring to a boil, then reduce the heat and simmer until the mixture reduces and is of a glaze consistency. Keep hot.

2 For the parsnip puree, steam the parsnips and potatoes until tender. Drain, if necessary, and place in a food processor or blender with the yogurt, horseradish (if using), and pepper to taste. Blend until combined. Keep warm or reheat prior to serving.

3 Brush the tuna with oil. Cook on a preheated, very hot grill pan or barbecue, or in a skillet or under a broiler, for 1–2 minutes. Turn and spoon the glaze over the tuna. Cook for another 1–2 minutes—it is best if moist and still slightly pink in the center.

4 To serve, top a mound of the puree with a tuna steak and spoon the remaining glaze over it. Accompany with steamed green vegetables, if you like.

4 tuna steaks, about 4 oz each
2 teaspoons olive oil

GLAZE
1 tablespoon honey
2 tablespoons whole-grain mustard
1 teaspoon tomato paste
2 tablespoons orange juice
1 tablespoon red wine vinegar or balsamic vinegar
freshly ground black pepper

PARSNIP PUREE
2 parsnips, cut into chunks
2 potatoes, cut into chunks
$\frac{1}{4}$ cup plain yogurt
2 teaspoons horseradish relish (optional)

NUTRITIONAL TIPS
Gilling is a healthy way to cook, since it requires little or no added fat, and any fat from the food can drain away. Grill pans can be heated to a very high heat, which gives food a delicious flavor and helps to seal in all the juices.

cod with chili lima beans & tomatoes

Preparation time: 15 minutes   **Serves 4**
Cooking time: 20 minutes
NUTRITIONAL FACTS   ◐ calories – 221 (930 kJ) ◐ Fat – 3 g, of which 0.5 g saturated ◐ Sodium – 408 mg

1 Heat the oil in a nonstick saucepan and add the celery, onion, and garlic. Cook for about 5 minutes until softened. Add the tomatoes, tomato paste, beans, and chili. Simmer, uncovered, for 10 minutes.

2 Meanwhile, heat the wine in a separate saucepan. Add the fish and poach gently for about 3–4 minutes, until just cooked through.

3 Combine the undrained fish with the bean and tomato mixture and heat through. Add pepper to taste, and garnish with parsley. Serve with new potatoes, basmati rice, or pasta, and spinach or broccoli for a feast of color.

2 teaspoons vegetable oil
1 celery stick, finely chopped
1 onion, finely chopped
1 garlic clove, crushed, or
    1 teaspoon minced garlic
13 oz canned tomatoes,
    undrained and mashed
2 tablespoons tomato paste
1¼ cups canned lima beans, well
    drained
1 green chili, seeded and finely
    chopped
½ cup dry white wine
1 lb cod fillet (or any boneless
    white fish fillets), cut
    into cubes
freshly ground black pepper
2 tablespoons chopped parsley,
    for garnishing

NUTRITIONAL TIPS
White fish such as cod, haddock, sand dab and sole, for example, are all low in calories, low in fat and saturated fat, and high in protein, minerals, and vitamins. So, although they are low in omega-3 fatty acids, they are to be valued just as much as oily fish to help you beat heart disease.

orange & cider poached mackerel

Preparation time: 15 minutes   **Serves 4**
Cooking time: 10 minutes

NUTRITIONAL FACTS   ● calories – 208 (875 kJ)   ● Fat – 4 g, of which 1 g saturated   ● Sodium – 144 mg

1 Heat the oil in a large nonstick saucepan, add the pepper, scallions, and ginger, and cook, stirring, for 1–2 minutes. Stir in the orange zest, cider, orange and lemon juices, and soy sauce. Bring to a boil.

2 Reduce the heat and add the fish. Cover and cook for 5 minutes, until the fish starts to flake when tested with a fork. Using a spatula or slotted spoon, remove the fish from the cooking liquid and place on a plate. Cover with foil. Keep warm in a low oven.

3 Add the cilantro and black pepper to the cooking liquid to taste. Bring to a boil. Boil rapidly until the mixture reduces to a sauce consistency. Serve with Tabbouleh (see page 44) or Baked Beets, Spinach, & Orange Salad (see page 42), if you like.

1 teaspoon olive oil
1 red bell pepper, cored, seeded, and finely chopped
2 scallions, sliced
1–2 inch piece of fresh ginger root, peeled and thinly sliced
1 teaspoon grated orange zest
½ cup hard cider
½ cup orange juice
2 tablespoons lemon juice
1 teaspoon reduced-salt soy sauce
4 mackerel fillets, about 5 oz each, skinned
2 tablespoons chopped fresh cilantro leaves
freshly ground black pepper

NUTRITIONAL TIPS
Keep a good supply of frozen fish, and other frozen food, in the freezer. They are just as nutritious as fresh foods in some cases and can act as the perfect healthy-eating, convenient way to cook your evening meal.

sea bass with mushroom & mixed herb stuffing

Preparation time: 15 minutes
Cooking time: 40 minutes

NUTRITIONAL FACTS   ○ calories – 310 (1200 kJ)   ○ Fat – 9 g, of which 1.5 g saturated   ○ Sodium – 105 mg

1 Heat 1 teaspoon of the oil in a nonstick skillet and gently cook the mushrooms for about 5 minutes until tender. Season to taste. Remove the pan from the heat and add the lemon zest and juice, and herbs.

2 Meanwhile, cook the potatoes in boiling water or a steamer for about 10 minutes, until just tender. Drain and let cool. Place the potatoes and garlic in a roasting pan, brush with most of the remaining oil, and roast in a preheated 400°F oven for about 20 minutes, until golden brown.

3 Make a crisscross incision on the skin side of the fish (to prevent the fish from curling). Make a cut lengthways down the side of each fillet into the center and pry open, creating a pocket for the stuffing. Brush with the remaining oil and stuff with the mushroom and herb mixture. Close the pocket to return the fish to its original shape.

4 Season with pepper to taste, and place on top of the potatoes. Return to the oven and bake for 5–6 minutes (depending upon size) until cooked through.

5 Serve with the fish placed on top of the potatoes and garnished with chopped herbs.

3 teaspoons olive oil
4 oz mixed mushrooms, preferably wild, sliced (about 1¼–1⅓ cups)
grated zest and juice of 1 lemon
handful of mixed herbs (such as flat-leaf parsley, thyme, or basil), roughly chopped
14 tiny new potatoes
1 garlic clove, crushed
2 sea bass or grouper fillets, about 4 oz each
freshly ground black pepper
chopped herbs, for garnishing

NUTRITIONAL TIPS
Sea bass and grouper contain a moderate amount of omega-3 fatty acids at 0.4 g per 3½-oz serving. The recommended amount is 1 g per day. You can add another 0.9 g of omega-3 to your meal by serving spinach with your fish. Spinach contains 0.9 g omega-3 fatty acids per 3½-oz serving.

creamy kedgeree with peas

Preparation time: 15 minutes

Serves 4

Cooking time: 15 minutes

NUTRITIONAL FACTS   ○ calories – 460 (1932 kJ)   ○ Fat – 8 g, of which 2 g saturated   ○ Sodium – 672 mg

1 Cook the rice following the instructions on the package. Place in a warmed serving dish.

2 Meanwhile, poach the fish in the milk in a pan for about 5 minutes, until just cooked. Strain, reserving the cooking liquid. Skin and flake the fish, removing any stray bones, and set aside.

3 In a separate small saucepan, heat the oil and add the scallions and curry paste. Cook gently for about 5 minutes until soft.

4 Combine the fish, rice, scallion mixture, peas, and chopped eggs in a large saucepan. Heat through, adding a little of the reserved cooking liquid if necessary. Season to taste with pepper.

5 Serve, garnished with tomatoes, parsley, and lemon wedges.

1⅓ cups basmati rice
8 oz haddock or any white fish
8 oz smoked haddock
2 cups lowfat milk
1 teaspoon olive oil
2 scallions, chopped
2 teaspoons curry paste
1 cup frozen peas, cooked
2 hard-cooked eggs, shelled and
    chopped
freshly ground black pepper

FOR GARNISHING
chopped tomatoes
chopped parsley
lemon wedges

NUTRITIONAL TIPS
Basmati rice has the lowest glycemic index (GI) of any rice. The GI of rice depends upon its amylose content—a type of starch that is broken down and absorbed relatively slowly by the body.

fisherman's pie with fresh spinach

Preparation time: 15 minutes

Cooking time: 40 minutes

Serves 4

NUTRITIONAL FACTS   ● calories – 360 (1512 kJ)   ● Fat – 11 g, of which 2 g saturated   ● Sodium – 822 mg

1 In a large pan, poach the fish in the milk with the bay leaf for 10 minutes, until tender. Strain, retaining the cooking liquid. Skin and flake the fish, removing any stray bones, and set aside.

2 Meanwhile, heat the oil in a small saucepan, add the onion and carrot, and cook gently for about 4 minutes. Steam the spinach and squeeze out any excess moisture.

3 Pour the fish-cooking liquid into a saucepan. Add the cornstarch paste and heat gently, stirring constantly, until thickened. Reduce the heat and simmer for at least 5 minutes. Remove from the heat. Add the mustard and season to taste with pepper.

4 Place the fish, egg quarters, and vegetables in an ovenproof dish. Pour the sauce over them. Top with the mashed potatoes. Bake in a preheated 350°F oven for 20 minutes.

5 Garnish with tomatoes and return to the oven for 5 minutes. Serve with peas or British baked beans, if you like.

1 lb white fish, such as a mixture of smoked and unsmoked cod or haddock

1¼ cups skim milk

1 bay leaf

1 teaspoon olive oil

1 onion, finely chopped

1 carrot, finely chopped

2 large handfuls of spinach leaves

1 tablespoon cornstarch, blended with a little cold water

1 teaspoon mustard

2 hard-cooked eggs, shelled and quartered

1 lb cooked potatoes, mashed with lowfat milk and unsaturated spread (about 2 cups)

freshly ground black pepper

sliced tomatoes, for garnishing

potato & olive bread

Preparation time: 25 minutes, plus proving
Cooking time: 40 minutes

(V)

Makes 1 loaf

NUTRITIONAL FACTS* · calories – 1840 (7801 kJ) · Fat – 23 g, of which 5 g saturated · Sodium – 1220 mg

1 Place the mashed potatoes in a large bowl with the flour. Blend the fresh yeast with the milk. If using dried yeast, dissolve the sugar in the milk, then sprinkle the yeast over it and leave in a warm place for about 10 minutes, until frothy. Add the yeast mixture and water to the potato and flour and mix to form a fairly firm dough.

2 Turn onto a floured counter and knead for about 10 minutes, until smooth and even. Shape into a ball, place inside an oiled plastic bag, and leave in a warm place until doubled in size.

3 Turn out the dough and knead until smooth, adding two thirds of the olives. Make into a loaf-like shape or shape to fit a greased 9 x 5 x 3-inch loaf pan. Cover with the oiled plastic bag and let rise in a warm place until the dough reaches the top of the pan. Remove the plastic bag and sprinkle the loaf with the remaining olives.

4 Bake in a preheated 425°F oven for about 40 minutes, either on a baking sheet if cooking it free-form or in the loaf pan, until the bottom of the loaf sounds hollow when tapped. Cool on a wire rack.

*figures for whole loaf

4 oz cooked potatoes, mashed
  with 1 tablespoon
  unsaturated spread (about
  ½ cup)
1 lb white bread flour (about
  3⅓–3¾ cups)
½ oz (1 tablespoon) fresh yeast
  or 1½ level teaspoons dried
  yeast plus 1 teaspoon sugar
⅔ cup warm milk
⅔ cup warm water
15 pitted black olives, thinly sliced

NUTRITIONAL TIPS
Bread can contain a surprising amount of salt, so by making your own you can limit the amount. This unusual bread contains a reasonable amount of salt because there are 70 mg sodium in each black olive. Rinse the olives and dry them thoroughly on paper towels before slicing them, to remove some of the salt.

garlic mash

Preparation time: 10 minutes

Cooking time: 1¼ hours

(V)   **Serves 4**

NUTRITIONAL FACTS   ● calories – 185 (777 kJ)   ● Fat – less than 1 g, of which a trace saturated   ● Sodium – 24 mg

1 Prick the potatoes with a fork and bake in a preheated 425°F oven for 1¼ hours until tender.

2 Meanwhile, remove the outer skin from the head of garlic but do not separate the cloves. Slice off the top. Wrap in foil, shiny side inwards. Place on a baking sheet and roast on a lower shelf in the oven for 45 minutes until the garlic flesh is softened to a puree.

3 Holding the baked potato with an oven mitt, pierce a cross in the top of each potato with a fork. Squeeze so that the flesh rises up through the skin. Scoop into a bowl and mash with a fork. (Save the crunchy skins for a snack.) Squeeze the roasted garlic flesh into the potatoes and mash thoroughly. Mix in the stock and milk, a tablespoon of each at a time, until the desired texture is achieved. Season to taste with pepper, then stir in the chives (if using).

OR YOU COULD TRY...

CHEESE MASH: Replace the stock and milk with 1–2 tablespoons plain fromage frais or yogurt and 2–3 tablespoons Parmesan cheese.

CELERY ROOT MASH: Mash potatoes with 12 oz peeled, chopped, and boiled celery root. Add skim milk, a little unsaturated spread and nutmeg.

1 firm head of garlic
3 baking potatoes, about 10 oz
    each, scrubbed
3–4 tablespoons warm
    Vegetable Stock (see
    page 122)
3–4 tablespoons warm skim
    milk
1 tablespoon chopped, fresh
    chives (optional)
freshly ground black pepper

NUTRITIONAL TIPS

Baked potatoes make the best mashed potatoes—smooth, rich, and creamy—and if you follow this recipe, they are surprisingly low in fat. The warm roasted garlic is also ideal for spreading right onto French bread.

simply baked potatoes

Preparation time: 5 minutes   (V)   **Serves 4**

Cooking time: 75 minutes

NUTRITIONAL FACTS* ● calories – 400 (1680 kJ) ● Fat – less than 1 g, of which negligible saturated ● Sodium – 36 mg

1 Bake the potatoes right on the rack of a preheated 425°F oven for 1¼ hours, until tender. You can shorten the cooking time by inserting a metal skewer into each potato, or by cutting the potato in half.

2 Slice open a cross in the top of each potato and fill with your choice of filling. Or cut the top off each potato and carefully scoop out most of the flesh. Mash with your choice of filling and pile it back into the skins. Serve now, or stand on a baking sheet and return to the oven or place under a medium broiler for 5 minutes, until reheated and beginning to brown.

OR YOU COULD TRY...

CURRIED SHRIMP AND ZUCCHINI TOPPING

Place 1 finely chopped onion with a little water in a saucepan over a low heat and cook for about 5 minutes, until soft. Stir in 1 teaspoon of turmeric, 2 tablespoons mild curry paste, 1 grated zucchini, 8 oz shrimps, and a little more water if necessary. Heat through gently. Use to top the baked potatoes when cooked. A serving of this topping would provide you with 100 calories, 2 g of fat of which less than 1 g is saturated, and 1109 mg of sodium in addition to the nutritional facts for each baked potato.

*figures for each 10 oz baked potato

4 baking potatoes in their skins,
    each 8–12 oz
a little vegetable oil (optional)
freshly ground black pepper

OR YOU COULD TRY...
More fillings and toppings:
● **Thai Beef and Pepper Stir-fry**
  (see page 100)
● **Smoked salmon (lox) and**
  chopped chives
● **Crispy lean bacon, apricots,**
  and celery
● **Grated low-fat cheese with**
  chopped shallots
● **Flaked tuna, corn, and plain**
  fromage frais
● **Shrimp with scallions and**
  plain yogurt
● **Cottage cheese with**
  pineapple

NUTRITIONAL TIPS
Baked potatoes have great nutritional value. They are a good source of both vitamin C and fiber, which is in their skins, so make sure you eat the crispy skin.

fettuccine with bacon, mushrooms, & pine nuts

Preparation time: 10 minutes

Serves 4

Cooking time: 10 minutes

NUTRITIONAL FACTS ● calories – 535 (2247 kJ) ● Fat – 14 g, of which 2 g saturated ● Sodium – 740 mg

1 Cook the fettuccine according to the package instructions.

2 Meanwhile, heat the oil in a nonstick skillet, add the pepper, and cook for 2–3 minutes. Stir in the garlic, mushrooms, cooked bacon, parsley, and pepper to taste.

3 Reduce the heat and stir in the fromage frais or yogurt. Heat through very gently.

4 Drain the pasta and toss with the sauce. Sprinkle with the toasted pine nuts before serving. Serve with an Italian-style salad and fresh ciabatta bread.

12 oz green and white fettuccine
1 tablespoon olive oil
1 yellow bell pepper, cored, seeded, and chopped
2 teaspoons garlic puree, or crushed garlic
4 oz button mushrooms, sliced (about 1¼ cups)
4 oz lean Canadian bacon (about 1 cup), broiled and cut into thin strips
1 tablespoon chopped parsley
2⅓ cups plain fromage frais or yogurt
3 tablespoons pine nuts, toasted
freshly ground black pepper

lean lasagne

Preparation time: 30 minutes

Cooking time: about 1 hour

Serves 8

NUTRITIONAL FACTS ● calories – 340 (1428 kJ) ● Fat – 11 g, of which 5 g saturated ● Sodium – 180 mg

1 Cook the lasagne sheets according to package instructions and set aside in a bowl of water until needed.

2 For the meat sauce, place the eggplants, onions, garlic, stock, and wine in a large nonstick pot. Cover and simmer briskly for 5 minutes.

3 Uncover and cook for about 5 minutes until the eggplant is tender and the liquid is absorbed, adding a little more stock if necessary. Remove from the heat, let cool slightly, then puree in a food processor or blender.

4 Meanwhile, brown the ground meat in a nonstick skillet. Drain off any fat. Add the eggplant mixture, tomatoes, and black pepper to taste. Simmer briskly, uncovered, for about 10 minutes, until thickened.

5 For the cheese sauce, beat the egg whites with the ricotta. Beat in the milk and 4 tablespoons of Parmesan. Season to taste with pepper.

6 To make the lasagne, alternate layers of the meat sauce, lasagne sheets, and cheese sauce. Start with meat sauce and finish with cheese sauce. Sprinkle with the remaining Parmesan. Bake in a preheated 350°F oven for 30–40 minutes, until browned.

7 oz lasagne

MEAT SAUCE
2 eggplants, peeled and cubed
2 red onions, chopped
2 garlic cloves, crushed
1¼ cups Vegetable Stock
   (see page 122)
¼ cup red wine
1 lb extra-lean ground beef
26 oz canned diced tomatoes
freshly ground black pepper

CHEESE SAUCE
3 egg whites
1 cup ricotta cheese
¾ cup skim milk
6 tablespoons freshly grated
   Parmesan cheese

NUTRITIONAL TIPS
Despite its Mediterranean origins, lasagne can be even higher in fat and calories than fried foods. In this reduced-fat version, the white sauce is made from low-fat ricotta cheese, which tastes sweet and creamy.

macaroni & cheese surprise

Preparation time: 15 minutes

Cooking time: 40 minutes

(V)   **Serves 4**

NUTRITIONAL FACTS   ○ calories – 308 (1293 kJ)   ○ Fat – 6 g, of which 3 g saturated   ○ Sodium – 255 mg

1 Cook the macaroni according to the package instructions until just tender, and drain.

2 Meanwhile, lightly cook in boiling water all the vegetables so that they remain crunchy. Drain well.

3 Mix the cornstarch and a little of the milk together in a saucepan. Blend to a smooth paste. Heat gently, adding the rest of the milk and whisking continuously until the sauce boils and thickens. Add three-quarters of the cheese, and the mustard and cayenne pepper to taste.

4 Mix together the cooked pasta and vegetables with the sauce, and spoon into an ovenproof dish. Scatter with the remaining cheese and sprinkle with a little cayenne pepper for the garnish. Bake in a preheated 400°F oven for about 25 minutes, until golden brown.

OR YOU COULD TRY...

Any vegetables, lightly cooked and added to the cheesy mixture, such as peas, corn, mixed bell peppers, carrots, mushrooms, and any other mixed vegetables.

1½ cups whole-wheat macaroni

2 carrots, cut into small, chunky sticks

8 oz broccoli florets (about 4–5 cups)

1 large leek, trimmed and sliced

½ cup cornstarch

2½ cups skim milk

1 cup low-fat sharp hard cheese, grated

1 teaspoon mustard

pinch of cayenne pepper, plus extra for garnishing

NUTRITIONAL TIPS

All pasta is naturally healthy—rich in carbohydrates and low in fat. Whole-wheat pasta is made from the whole grain and contains more insoluble fiber than the white pastas. This type of fiber helps to prevent constipation and other bowel problems.

bow ties with anchovy & oregano sauce

Preparation time: 10 minutes **Serves 4**

Cooking time: 15 minutes

NUTRITIONAL FACTS ○ calories – 390 (1653 kJ) ○ Fat – 7 g, of which less than 1 g saturated ○ Sodium – 500 mg

1 Heat the oil in a small saucepan, add the garlic, and fry gently for about 5 minutes, until golden.

2 Reduce the heat to very low, stir in the anchovies, and cook very gently for about 10 minutes, until they have completely disintegrated.

3 Meanwhile, cook the pasta according to the package instructions, until just tender.

4 Stir the oregano, and pepper to taste, into the sauce.

5 Drain the pasta and turn into a warmed serving dish. Pour the sauce over it, sprinkle with the parsley, and gently toss together. Serve with Parmesan cheese and a crisp Mediterranean salad, if you like.

1 tablespoon olive oil

2 garlic cloves, finely chopped

2 oz canned anchovy fillets (about 1/4 cup), drained

12 oz dried bow ties (5 1/2–6 cups)

2 teaspoons fresh oregano, finely chopped

3 tablespoons chopped parsley

freshly ground black pepper

grated Parmesan cheese, for serving

NUTRITIONAL TIPS

All pasta has a very low glycemic index (GI). This is because it is made from high-protein semolina (finely cracked wheat) and has a dense food matrix that resists disruption in the small intestine. But even pasta made from fine flour instead of semolina has a relatively low GI. Interestingly, there is some evidence that thicker pasta has a lower GI than thin varieties.

wild rice jambalaya

Preparation time: 15 minutes

Cooking time: 35 minutes

NUTRITIONAL FACTS   ○ calories – 370 (1554 kJ)   ○ Fat – 3 g, of which less than 1 g saturated   ○ Sodium – 680 mg

Serves 4

1 Place the wild rice in a saucepan with water to cover. Bring to a boil and boil for 5 minutes. Remove the pan from the heat and cover tightly. Let it steam in its heat for about 10 minutes until the grains are tender. Drain.

2 Heat the oil in a large nonstick skillet. Add the celery, peppers, onion, bacon, and garlic. Cook, stirring, for 3–4 minutes, until the vegetables are soft. Stir in the tomato paste and thyme. Cook for another 2 minutes.

3 Add the cooked wild rice, and the long-grain rice, chili, cayenne pepper, pimientos (if using), tomatoes, stock, and wine. Bring to a boil. Reduce the heat and simmer for 10 minutes, until the rice is tender but still firm to the bite.

4 Add the shrimp or mycoprotein and cook, stirring occasionally, for 5 minutes, until the shrimp have turned opaque. Spoon into large warmed bowls. Scatter with cilantro or parsley, and serve. Accompany with crusty bread, if you like.

²/₃ cup wild rice

1 teaspoon olive oil

scant ¹/₂ cup chopped celery

¹/₂ red bell pepper, cored, seeded, and chopped

¹/₂ green or yellow bell pepper, cored, seeded and chopped

1 onion, chopped

1 slice lean Canadian bacon, trimmed of fat

2 garlic cloves, crushed

2 tablespoons tomato paste

1 tablespoon chopped fresh thyme

²/₃ cup long-grain rice

1 green chili, seeded and finely chopped

¹/₂ teaspoon cayenne pepper

1 tablespoon chopped canned pimientos (optional)

13 oz canned tomatoes, drained

1¹/₄ cups Chicken Stock (see page 122)

²/₃ cup dry white wine

8 oz raw medium shrimp or mycoprotein pieces

3 tablespoons chopped fresh cilantro or parsley, for garnishing

chicken, wild mushroom, & fennel rice

Preparation time: 10 minutes

Cooking time: 30 minutes

NUTRITIONAL FACTS   calories – 440 (1848 kJ)   Fat – 10 g, of which 1 g saturated   Sodium – 260 mg

Serves 4

1 Heat the oil in a saucepan and gently fry the fennel, onion, and garlic for 5 minutes. Add the mushrooms and cook for 2 minutes. Stir in the rice and gently fry for 2 minutes. Add the wine and stir until absorbed by the rice.

2 Add half the stock and bring to a boil, then lower the heat and simmer gently, stirring frequently, until absorbed. Add the rest of the stock, a little at a time, allowing each amount to be absorbed before adding the next.

3 After about 15 minutes, add the chicken, dill weed, and lemon zest and juice. Cook for about 5 minutes more, until the rice is creamy but still firm to the bite. Season to taste with pepper and turn into a warmed serving dish. Sprinkle with pine nuts and garnish with dill weed sprigs.

1 tablespoon olive oil

1 fennel bulb, trimmed and finely sliced

1 onion, finely sliced

1 garlic clove, crushed

6 oz mixed and wild mushrooms, sliced (about 1¾–2 cups)

1⅓ cups basmati rice

⅔ cup dry white wine

2 cups Chicken Stock (see page 122)

8 oz cooked chicken, chopped (about 1½ cups)

½ bunch of dill weed, chopped

finely grated zest and juice of 1 lemon

freshly ground black pepper

3 tablespoons pine nuts, toasted

dill weed sprigs, for garnishing

NUTRITIONAL TIPS

Traditional Asian-style diets, characterized by relatively large quantities of rice and small quantities of meat, offer many heart-health benefits. Paella mirrors this principle and can be made with a variety of ingredients such as vegetables, fish, and meat.

red kidney bean & eggplant pilaf

Preparation time: 15 minutes

Cooking time: 40 minutes

(V)   **Serves 4**

NUTRITIONAL FACTS   ❍ calories – 330 (1386 kJ)   ❍ Fat – 7 g, of which 1 g saturated   ❍ Sodium – 144 mg

1 Place the water in a large pan and bring to a boil. Add the rice and turmeric and stir well to prevent the rice from sticking. Cover, and simmer for 30 minutes without stirring. Remove from the heat.

2 Meanwhile, heat the oil in a nonstick skillet, add the onion, garlic, celery, pepper, and eggplant, and cook gently for 3 minutes, without browning. Add the tomatoes and mushrooms, stir well, and cook for 3–4 minutes.

3 Stir the beans and the vegetable mixture into the cooked rice, cover, and cook very gently for 10 minutes.

4 Remove from the heat and let sit for 5 minutes. Season to taste with pepper and stir in the parsley. Transfer to a warmed serving dish for serving.

OR YOU COULD TRY...

Adding 18 oz cooked, chopped chicken (about 3–3½ cups) before the tomatoes and mushrooms, for an alternative non-vegetarian supper.

2 cups water
1⅓ cups brown long-grain rice
½ teaspoon turmeric
1 tablespoon vegetable oil
1 large onion, finely chopped
1 garlic clove, finely chopped
1 celery stick, chopped
1 green bell pepper, cored, seeded, and chopped
1 eggplant, cubed
2 tomatoes, skinned and chopped
4 oz mushrooms, sliced (about 1¼ cups)
1⅓ cups canned kidney beans, rinsed and drained
2 tablespoons chopped parsley
freshly ground black pepper

NUTRITIONAL TIPS

Beans are a good source of protein, especially when they are served with a cereal food such as rice, bread, or pasta. They are low in fat, high in fiber, and rich in many nutrients, providing iron, zinc, calcium, folate, and soluble fiber.

tomato & herb scone pie

Preparation time: 15 minutes   (V)   **Serves 6**

Cooking time: 35–40 minutes

NUTRITIONAL FACTS   O calories – 340 (1428 kJ)   O Fat – 15g, of which 5 g saturated   O Sodium – 268 mg

1 For the scone base, sift the dry ingredients into a mixing bowl and rub in the spread until the mixture resembles fine bread crumbs. Add just enough milk to form a soft dough. Turn out onto a lightly floured counter and knead until smooth. Roll out to a 9–10-inch diameter circle, then place on a greased baking sheet.

2 For the topping, heat the oil in a large pan, add the onion and garlic, and fry gently for 5 minutes, until softened. Add the pepper, tomatoes, tomato paste, and basil or thyme, and simmer, uncovered, for about 10 minutes, until the mixture is thick. Season with black pepper.

3 Spread the tomato mixture over the base right to the edge. Top with the cheese. Bake in the center of a preheated 425°F oven for 20–25 minutes, until the topping is bubbling.

OR YOU COULD TRY...

- O Anchovy fillets and black olives
- O Red onion, feta cheese, red bell pepper, and arugula
- O Spinach and ricotta
- O Caponata Ratatouille (see page 48)

SCONE BASE

- 2 cups whole-wheat flour
- 1 tablespoon baking powder
- ¼ teaspoon salt
- 3½ tablespoons unsaturated spread
- ⅔ cup skim milk

TOPPING

- 1 tablespoon olive oil
- 2 large onions, chopped
- 1–2 garlic cloves
- 1 red bell pepper, cored, seeded, and sliced
- 26 oz canned tomatoes
- 2 tablespoons tomato paste
- handful basil or thyme, chopped
- 4 oz low-fat mozzarella cheese, sliced (about 1 cup)
- freshly ground black pepper

NUTRITIONAL TIPS

Homemade pizzas, like this scone pie, can be very healthy, with a starchy base topped with your own choice of fresh vegetables and low-fat ingredients. Look out for half-fat mozzarella, which has only 10 g of fat per cup.

thai sesame & tofu stir-fry

Preparation time: 15 minutes
Cooking time: 10 minutes

(V)   **Serves 4**

NUTRITIONAL FACTS   ○ calories – 400 (1680 kJ)   ○ Fat – 12 g, of which 2 g saturated   ○ Sodium – 400 mg

1 In a small bowl, mix together the sesame oil and 1 tablespoon Teriyaki Sauce. Brush the mixture over both sides of the tofu. Sprinkle one side of each piece of tofu with half the sesame seeds. Mix together the remaining Teriyaki Sauce, vinegar, and soy sauce. Set aside.

2 Heat a large wok or skillet. Brush with a little of the peanut oil. Add the tofu, seed side down, and cook for 2 minutes. Sprinkle the remaining sesame seeds over the tofu. Turn over and cook for 2 minutes more until crisp. Remove the tofu from the pan and keep warm.

3 Brush the pan with a little more peanut oil, then add the snow peas, carrot, bean sprouts, and scallion lengths. Stir-fry for 2–3 minutes until tender yet still crisp. Add the reserved teriyaki sauce mixture. Stir-fry for 1 minute.

4 Meanwhile, cook the noodles according to the package instructions. Divide the hot noodles between warmed serving bowls. Add the watercress, spoon the vegetables over them, and top with the tofu. Garnish with the green shredded scallions. Serve with a green salad, if you like.

1 teaspoon sesame oil

2 tablespoons Teriyaki Sauce (see page 124)

13 oz firm tofu, cut into 4 thick slices

2 tablespoons sesame seeds

1 tablespoon rice wine vinegar

2 teaspoons low-salt soy sauce

1 tablespoon peanut oil

16 snow peas

1 carrot, cut into thin strips

4 oz bean sprouts (about 2 cups)

2 scallions, white parts cut into 2-inch lengths, green tops shredded for garnish

8 oz rice stick noodles

2 oz watercress sprigs (about 1–1¼ cups)

NUTRITIONAL TIPS
Tofu (soybean curd) is rich in protein and B vitamins, low in saturated fat and sodium, and an important non-dairy source of calcium.

vegetarian cider & sage sausages

Preparation time: 10 minutes
Cooking time: 35–45 minutes

(V)

Serves 4

NUTRITIONAL FACTS   ● calories – 200 (840 kJ)   ● Fat – 3.5 g, of which 2 g saturated   ● Sodium – 200 mg

1 Heat a heavy pan. Add the sausages and cook for 8–10 minutes, turning frequently, until browned all over. Remove and set aside.

2 Pour a little water into the pan, add the vegetables, and simmer gently for about 5 minutes, stirring, until lightly colored. Stir in the flour and cook for 1–2 minutes.

3 Pour in the cider and stock and bring to a boil, stirring. Reduce the heat and return the sausages to the pan. Season to taste with pepper and add the sage. Cover and cook for 20–30 minutes, stirring occasionally, adding a little more stock if necessary. Serve with Garlic Mash (see page 72), if you like.

6 vegetarian or mycoprotein
    (Quorn) sausages
1 onion, sliced
2 celery sticks, sliced
2 carrots, sliced
1 green bell pepper, cored,
    seeded, and sliced
2 tablespoons flour
1¼ cups hard cider
¾–1¼ cups homemade
    Vegetable Stock (see
    page 122)
1 teaspoon dried sage
freshly ground black pepper

easy bean & pepper casserole

Preparation time: 10 minutes

Cooking time: 30–40 minutes

(V)   **Serves 4**

NUTRITIONAL FACTS   ● calories – 384 (1613 kJ)   ● Fat – 25 g, of which 2 g saturated   ● Sodium – 586 mg

1 In a large bowl, mix together all the beans, tomatoe puree, onion, herbs, garlic, fennel or celery, peppers, and black pepper to taste.

2 Brush an ovenproof dish with a little oil. Pour in the bean mixture and top with the chopped tomatoes.

3 Bake in a preheated 350°F oven for 35–40 minutes. Serve sprinkled with Parmesan. Accompany with wild rice, broccoli, and steamed carrots and parsnips, if you like.

1 cup canned cranberry beans, rinsed and drained

1½ cups canned lima beans, rinsed and drained

1½ cups canned flageolet beans, rinsed and drained

1¾ cups tomato puree

1 large onion, chopped

2 teaspoons dried Italian herbs

2 teaspoons chopped parsley

1 garlic clove, finely chopped

1 bulb of fennel, or celery, sliced

2 red or green bell peppers, cored, seeded, and chopped

a little vegetable oil, for brushing

2 tomatoes, chopped

freshly ground black pepper

3 tablespoons grated Parmesan cheese, for serving

NUTRITIONAL TIPS

Beans are high in soluble and insoluble fiber. Soluble fiber helps lower blood cholesterol and control blood sugar levels, while insoluble fiber helps to prevent bowel problems.

mixed masala beans

Preparation time: 5 minutes
Cooking time: 30 minutes

(V)   **Serves 4**

NUTRITIONAL FACTS   ○ calories – 150 (630 kJ)   ○ Fat – 5 g, of which 0.5 g saturated   ○ Sodium – 315 mg

1 Heat the oil in a heavy pan, add the onion and cumin seeds, and fry gently for about 5 minutes until lightly golden. Stir in the other spices. Add the 2 tablespoons water and cook, stirring continuously, for 1–2 minutes.

2 Gently stir in the chickpeas, kidney beans, tomato, chilies, garlic, and ginger. Mix well and stir in the cup of water. Bring to a boil, then reduce the heat and simmer for 15–20 minutes.

3 Add the pepper and cook for another 2–3 minutes. Stir in the lemon juice and half the cilantro. Serve immediately, garnished with the remaining cilantro.

OR YOU COULD TRY...
Serving this versatile dish with basmati rice and a crisp green salad, or as a vegetable side dish with Tandoori Chicken (see page 104) or Kofta Curry (see page 106), or as a topping for baked potatoes (see page 73), or cold as a salad.

1 tablespoon vegetable oil
1 small onion, chopped
½ teaspoon cumin seeds
½ teaspoon chili powder
½ teaspoon turmeric
¼ teaspoon garam masala
1 cup water, plus 2 tablespoons
¾ cup canned chickpeas, rinsed
  and drained
¾ cup canned red kidney beans,
  rinsed and drained
1 tomato, chopped
1–2 green chilies, seeded and
  chopped
4 garlic cloves, finely chopped
1 teaspoon finely grated fresh
  ginger root
1 green bell pepper, cored,
  seeded, and chopped
2 teaspoons lemon juice
2–3 tablespoons fresh cilantro
  leaves, chopped

NUTRITIONAL TIPS
Beans are an excellent source of phytoestrogens which possess antiviral, antibacterial, anticarcinogenic, and antifungal properties.

chili bean & corn stuffed peppers

Preparation time: 15 minutes
Cooking time: about 1 hour

(V)

Serves 4

NUTRITIONAL FACTS   ● calories – 300 (1260 kJ)   ● Fat – 7g, of which 2 g saturated   ● Sodium – 425 mg

1 Place the rice in a large pan of cold water and bring to a boil. Reduce the heat and simmer for 20–25 minutes, until tender. Drain and place in a bowl.

2 Meanwhile, pour the oil in a pan, add the onion, and fry gently for 5 minutes. Add this to the rice along with the chili powder, corn, and beans. Season to taste with pepper.

3 Slice the tops off the peppers and set aside. Shave a little off the bottoms so that they sit upright, then remove and discard the cores and seeds. Stand the peppers on a baking sheet.

4 Stir the cheese into the rice mixture and pile into the peppers, packing down well. Replace the pepper tops. Bake in a preheated 400°F oven for 30 minutes, until tender. Serve with plain yogurt, if you like.

OR YOU COULD TRY...
Using this filling to stuff the following vegetables: eggplants, onions, mushrooms, potatoes, acorn squash, butternut squash, tomatoes, savoy cabbage leaves, vine leaves, and zucchini.

generous 1/3 cup easy-cook brown rice
1 tablespoon vegetable oil
1 onion, finely chopped
1/2 teaspoon hot chili powder
7 oz canned corn (about 1 1/3–1 1/2 cups), rinsed and drained
7 oz canned kidney beans (about 1 1/3 cups), rinsed and drained
4 red bell peppers
1/2 cup grated low-fat sharp hard cheese
freshly ground black pepper
plain yogurt, for serving

NUTRITIONAL TIPS
Highly convenient to use, canned legumes, baked beans, corn, and peas, are essential items for your healthy-heart cupboard. By adding beans to any of your dishes, you can help reduce your risk of heart disease.

tomato & mushroom soy ragù

Preparation time: 15 minutes

Cooking time: 20–25 minutes

NUTRITIONAL FACTS   ● calories – 195 (819 kJ)   ● Fat – 5 g, of which 0.5g saturated   ● Sodium – 2011 mg

V   **Serves 4**

1 Prepare the dried soy according to the package instructions.

2 Heat the oil in a large pan, add the onion and garlic, and cook, stirring, for 2–3 minutes, until softened.

3 Add the mushrooms, carrot, tomatoes, stock, tomato paste, herbs, yeast extract, prepared soy mixture, and pepper to taste. Stir well, then simmer for 20–25 minutes.

4 Meanwhile, cook the spaghetti according to the package instructions, until just tender. Drain well.

5 Serve the spaghetti topped with the sauce and sprinkled with a little Parmesan. Accompany with a green leafy salad, if you like.

5 oz dried soy meat-substitute
1 tablespoon vegetable oil
1 onion, chopped
1 garlic clove, crushed
4 oz mushrooms, sliced (about 1¼ cups)
1 carrot, sliced
2 lb ripe tomatoes, skinned, or 26 oz canned diced tomatoes
²/₃ cup Vegetable Stock (see page 122)
2 tablespoons tomato paste
1 teaspoon dried oregano
1 teaspoon dried basil
1 teaspoon yeast extract (or crumbled beef bouillion cube)
13 oz dried spaghetti
freshly ground black pepper
grated Parmesan cheese, for serving

cashew & green pepper risotto

Preparation time: 5 minutes
Cooking time: 55 minutes

(V)   **Serves 5**

NUTRITIONAL FACTS   ○ calories – 421 (1768 kJ)   ○ Fat – 16 g, of which 3 g saturated   ○ Sodium – 410 mg

1 Heat the oil in a large skillet or wok, add the onion and pepper, and fry gently for about 5 minutes, until softened. Add the corn and rice, and cook, stirring, for 1 minute.

2 Stir in the stock and bring to a boil. Reduce the heat and simmer, uncovered, for 30–40 minutes, until the rice is tender.

3 Stir in the soy sauce and cashews and cook for another 5–10 minutes, until all the stock is absorbed. Serve with a mixed salad, if you like, or as a side dish.

2 teaspoons vegetable oil

1 onion, finely sliced

1 green bell pepper, cored, seeded, and finely sliced

1 cup corn

1½ cups brown rice

3¾ cups hot Vegetable Stock (see page 122)

1 tablespoon reduced-salt soy sauce

1 cup unsalted cashews

NUTRITIONAL TIPS
Research suggests that eating a small handful of unsalted nuts (1 oz/about ¼ cup) on most days can lower cholesterol and reduce the risk of a heart attack. Although high in fat, nuts make a healthy substitute for snacks like potato chips and cookies.

lentil & vegetable khichiri

Preparation time: 10 minutes, plus soaking
Cooking time: 35 minutes

(V)

Serves 4

NUTRITIONAL FACTS ● calories – 300 (1260 kJ) ● Fat – 8 g, of which 1 g saturated ● Sodium – 26 mg

1 Wash the lentils and rice together, then soak in a bowl of water for 15–20 minutes. Drain and set aside.

2 Heat the oil in a pan, add the onion, cinnamon, cardamom (if using), cumin seeds, and cloves, and fry gently for about 5 minutes, stirring frequently, until the onion turns a deep golden color.

3 Add the turmeric, chili powder, ginger and garlic paste, yogurt, and a little water, and cook for 2–3 minutes, adding a little more water if necessary. Stir in the beans, carrot, and tomato, and cook for 1–2 minutes.

4 Add the soaked rice and lentils, stir to mix, then add the measured water. Cover the pan with a close-fitting lid and bring to a boil. Reduce the heat and simmer for 20 minutes, then let stand for 3–4 minutes before serving.

¼ cup red lentils
1 cup basmati or long-grain rice
2 tablespoons vegetable oil
1 onion, finely chopped
½-inch piece cinnamon stick
1 black cardamom pod, split or bruised (optional)
1 teaspoon cumin seeds
2–3 cloves
¼ teaspoon turmeric
½ teaspoon chili powder
2 teaspoons Ginger and Garlic Paste (see page 123)
1 tablespoon plain yogurt
3 oz green beans, chopped (about ½–¾ cup)
3 oz carrot, chopped (about ½–¾ cup)
½ small tomato, chopped
2 cups water

NUTRITIONAL TIPS

Legumes including lentils, chickpeas, soybeans, and kidney beans are an important part of a low glycemic index (GI) diet. It is recommended that you try to eat beans—either dried or canned—at least twice a week.

eggplant & potato soy moussaka

Preparation time: 45 minutes

Cooking time: 45 minutes

(V)

Serves 4

NUTRITIONAL FACTS   ● calories – 445 (2226 kJ) ● Fat – 12g, of which 4 g saturated ● Sodium – 1932 mg

1 Heat most of the oil in a nonstick skillet and fry the eggplant in batches for about 10 minutes, until lightly browned. Set aside. Repeat with the potato slices, carefully adding a little boiling water or stock if necessary. Set aside.

2 Add the onion to the pan and cook for 5 minutes. Add the prepared soy and cook for 5 minutes. Add the wine, stock, tomato puree and paste, spices, thyme, and pepper to taste. Gently simmer, uncovered, for about 15 minutes, until thickened. Remove from the heat.

3 For the topping, blend the cornstarch with a little of the milk. Place in a saucepan over a low heat and gradually whisk in the remaining milk. Continue stirring until the sauce thickens. Simmer for 2–3 minutes. Stir in the nutmeg and let cool before whisking in the egg.

4 Brush an ovenproof dish with the remaining oil. Place a layer of potato in the bottom, cover with a layer of the sauce, followed by a layer of eggplant. Continue layering in this order. Pour the topping over the dish and sprinkle with Parmesan. Bake in a preheated 375°F oven for about 45 minutes, until browned.

1 tablespoon olive oil

2 medium eggplants, thinly sliced

2 large potatoes, thinly sliced

1 large onion, chopped

5 oz dried soy meat-substitute, prepared according to package instructions

1¼ cups red wine

1¼ cups Vegetable Stock (see page 122)

1¼ cups tomato puree

2 tablespoons tomato paste

½ teaspoon ground cinnamon

¼ teaspoon ground nutmeg

½ teaspoon dried thyme

freshly ground black pepper

¼ cup cornstarch

2 cups skim milk

¼ teaspoon ground nutmeg

1 egg

2 oz Parmesan cheese, grated (about ⅔–¾ cup)

NUTRITIONAL TIPS

To reduce the amount of oil used in frying vegetables, add a little hot stock or wine or sherry so that they sauté or steam in their own juices.

sweet potato & cannellini falafel

Preparation time: 20 minutes   **V**   **Serves 6**

Cooking time: 10 minutes

NUTRITIONAL FACTS   ◗ calories – 215 (903 kJ)   ◗ Fat – 8 g, of which 1 g saturated   ◗ Sodium – 245 mg

1 Boil or microwave the sweet potato until tender, then drain. Place in a bowl and mash. Set aside.

2 Heat the oil in a nonstick skillet, add the garlic, cumin, and ground coriander. Cook, stirring, for 1–2 minutes until fragrant. Stir in the tomato paste. Cook for 3–4 minutes until the mixture becomes deep red and develops a rich aroma. Stir in the beans.

3 Place the fresh cilantro, tahini, and lemon juice in a food processor or blender and blend to form a coarse paste.

4 Mix the bean mixture and bread crumbs with the sweet potato. Shape the mixture into 1-inch round patties. If the mixture feels too wet to shape into patties, you may need to add some extra bread crumbs. Roll in flour to coat. Place on a plate lined with plastic wrap. Cover and refrigerate until ready to cook—the patties can be made up to 1 day in advance.

5 Broil the falafel under a preheated hot broiler for 3–4 minutes each side, until golden and crispy.

6 Spread the bread with hummus. Top with lettuce, tabbouleh, and onion. Place 3 falafel in each pita and flatten slightly. Sprinkle with lemon juice to taste and serve immediately.

6 pita breads, warmed
1 tablespoon low-fat hummus or Tahini Hummus (see page 29)
3½ oz shredded lettuce (about 2 cups)
1¾ cups Tabbouleh (see page 44)
1 red onion, thinly sliced
lemon juice, for serving

FALAFEL

13 oz orange sweet potato, cut into chunks (about 3 cups)
2 teaspoons olive oil
1 clove garlic, crushed
2 teaspoons ground cumin
1 teaspoon ground coriander
1 tablespoon tomato paste
1½ cups canned cannellini beans, rinsed and drained
2 tablespoons chopped fresh cilantro leaves
1 tablespoon tahini (sesame seed paste)
1 tablespoon lemon juice
3 oz dry breadcrumbs (about 1 cup)
flour, for coating

thai beef & mixed pepper stir-fry

Preparation time: 20 minutes

Serves 4

Cooking time: 10 minutes

NUTRITIONAL FACTS* ○ calories – 255 (1067 kJ) ○ Fat – 12 g, of which 3 g saturated ○ Sodium – 4 mg

1 Cut the beef into long, thin strips, cutting across the grain.

2 Heat the oil in a wok or large skillet over high heat. Add the garlic and stir-fry for 1 minute.

3 Add the beef and stir-fry for 2–3 minutes, until lightly colored. Stir in the lemon grass and ginger and remove the pan from the heat. Remove the beef from the pan and set side.

4 Add the peppers and onion and stir-fry for 2–3 minutes, until the onions are just turning golden brown and are slightly softened.

5 Return the beef to the pan, stir in the lime juice, and season to taste with pepper. Serve with boiled noodles or rice, if you like.

1 lb lean beef tenderloin

1 tablespoon sesame oil

1 garlic clove, finely chopped

1 lemon grass stalk, finely
    shredded

1-inch piece of fresh ginger root,
    peeled and finely chopped

1 red bell pepper, cored, seeded,
    and thickly sliced

1 green bell pepper, cored,
    seeded, and thickly sliced

1 onion, thickly sliced

2 tablespoons lime juice

freshly ground black pepper

*figures per serving without noodles or rice

NUTRITIONAL TIPS

Stir-frying is a healthy and easy way to cook. It is important to measure the oil by the teaspoon or tablespoon and use the minimum amount necessary. You can stir-fry in water, stock, or wine to reduce the fat content further.

cranberry & orange turkey fillets

Preparation time: 5 minutes   **Serves 4**
Cooking time: 45–50 minutes
NUTRITIONAL FACTS   ○ calories – 330 (1386 kJ)   ○ Fat – 2 g, of which less than 1 g saturated   ○ Sodium – 120 mg

1 In a small bowl, mix together the honey, orange juice and zest, allspice, and cranberries.

2 Remove all visible fat from the turkey breasts. Place in an ovenproof dish and pour half the cranberry mixture over the turkey. Bake in a preheated 375°F oven for 15 minutes.

3 Remove the dish from the oven, turn the turkey pieces, and pour the remaining sauce over them. Return to the oven for another 30–35 minutes. Serve with Spiced Roast Roots (see page 52) or baked potatoes and green leafy vegetables, if you like.

2 teaspoons honey
1¼ cups orange juice
1 teaspoon grated orange zest
½ teaspoon ground allspice
1 lb cranberries (about 5 cups),
    fresh, canned, or frozen
    and thawed
4 boneless, skinless turkey
    breast fillets, about 4 oz each

NUTRITIONAL TIPS
Even when cooking lean meat such as poultry, be sure to remove the fat-laden skin and trim away all the visible fat. The white meat contains less fat than the dark meat, but avoid overcooking the white meat, since it tends to dry out. Keep moist by basting with stock and wine. In many recipes, chicken and turkey can easily be substituted for other lean meats, such as rabbit, venison, and ostrich.

chicken enchiladas with mango salsa

Preparation time: 20 minutes

Cooking time: 25 minutes

Serves 6

NUTRITIONAL FACTS* ● calories – 240 (1048 kJ) ● Fat – 3 g, of which less than 1 g saturated ● Sodium – 190mg

1 Heat the oil in a pan, add the onion, and cook for about 5 minutes, until softened. Stir in the beans, chicken, chilies, oregano, and fresh tomato. Heat through, then remove from the heat.

2 Place the chili powder, cumin, and blended tomatoes or tomato puree in a saucepan and simmer for 2 minutes. Remove from the heat.

3 Dip each tortilla into the tomato mixture and set aside on a plate. Fill each tortilla with 3 tablespoons of the chicken mixture. Roll up and place, seam-side down, in an ovenproof dish. Pour two thirds of the mango salsa over the enchiladas. Sprinkle with the cheese.

4 Bake in a preheated 350°F oven for about 20 minutes. Place 2 enchiladas on each plate and serve with the remaining salsa.

2 teaspoons vegetable oil

1 large onion, chopped

1²/₃ cups canned pinto beans, rinsed and drained

10 oz cooked chicken breast, skinned and cubed (about 2 cups)

4 green chilies, seeded and chopped

1 teaspoon dried oregano

1 large tomato, chopped

¼ teaspoon chili powder

¼ teaspoon ground cumin

13 oz canned tomatoes, blended in a food processor or strained, or 1³/₄ cups tomato puree

12 corn tortillas

quantity of Mango Salsa (see page 125)

²/₃ cup grated low-fat mozzarella cheese

*figures per enchilada

tandoori chicken

Preparation time: 10 minutes, plus marinating   **Serves 5**

Cooking time: 20 minutes

NUTRITIONAL FACTS   **○** calories – 212 (890 kJ) **○** Fat –4 g, of which 1 g saturated **○** Sodium – 110 mg

1 Mix together all the ingredients for the marinade in a bowl.

2 Place the chicken in a non-metallic dish. Spoon the marinade over it and rub well into the chicken. Cover and refrigerate for 2–4 hours.

3 Scrape the excess marinade from the chicken and discard it. Place the chicken on a wire rack set in a roasting tray. Pour in wine or water to the depth of 1 inch and add the herb sprigs, to keep the meat moist during cooking.

4 Bake the chicken in a preheated 475°F oven for 10 minutes. Turn over and bake for another 10 minutes until cooked through. Serve with Herbed Yogurt and Cucumber Sauce (see page 140), and accompany with nan bread, basmati rice, and a green salad, if you like.

4 boneless, skinless chicken breasts, about 5 oz each
wine or water
a few herb sprigs, such as rosemary, thyme, or parsley

MARINADE
1 tablespoon grated fresh ginger root
2 teaspoons coriander seeds, toasted
2 teaspoons dried rosemary leaves
1 teaspoon grated lemon zest
$\frac{1}{2}$ teaspoon ground cardamom
$\frac{1}{2}$ teaspoon ground cumin
$\frac{1}{4}$ teaspoon crushed black peppercorns
$\frac{1}{4}$ teaspoon chili sauce or powder
generous $\frac{1}{2}$ cup plain yogurt
1 tablespoon lemon juice

> ### NUTRITIONAL TIPS
> *The tandoori marinade and cooking method involves no added fat or sugar and can also be used for fish or lamb. Fish can be cooked on a grillpan or in a broiler for 3 minutes each side.*

turkish lamb & potato stew

Preparation time: 20 minutes
Cooking time: 2 hours

NUTRITIONAL FACTS   ● calories – 307 (1290 kJ)   ● Fat – 10 g, of which 4 g saturated   ● Sodium – 384 mg

1 Heat the oil in a large, heavy pan. Add the lamb and fry, stirring, until sealed and browned all over.

2 Add the onions and garlic and fry gently for about 5 minutes, until softened. Add the potatoes, tomatoes, pepper, stock or water, and vinegar, and bring to a boil. Add the herbs and season well with pepper. Cover and simmer gently for 1 hour.

3 Stir well, then add the eggplant and/or fennel and olives. Return to a boil, cover, and simmer gently for 45–60 minutes, until the lamb is very tender, stirring occasionally. Discard the bay leaves before serving. Serve with pita bread and a mixed salad, if you like.

1 tablespoon vegetable oil
1 lb lean lamb, cut into
   $3/4$-inch cubes (about 2 cups)
4 onions, cut into wedges
2 garlic cloves, crushed
$1\frac{1}{2}$ lb potatoes, cut into chunks
   (about $4\frac{1}{2}$–$5\frac{1}{4}$ cups)
12 oz tomatoes, skinned and
   sliced or quartered (about
   2–$2\frac{1}{2}$ cups)
1 red or green bell pepper, cored,
   seeded, and sliced
$3\frac{3}{4}$ cups stock or water
2 tablespoons wine vinegar
2 bay leaves
1 teaspoon chopped fresh sage
1 tablespoon chopped dill weed
1 eggplant and/or 1 chopped
   fennel bulb
12 pitted black olives
freshly ground black pepper

NUTRITIONAL TIPS
Beef, pork, and lamb can all be part of a healthy heart diet providing the meat is extremely lean. Only eat small amounts and accompany with plenty of beans, vegetables, and carbohydrates.

kofta curry

Preparation time: 25 minutes, plus chilling   **Serves 4**
Cooking time: 40 minutes
NUTRITIONAL FACTS   ⊙ calories – 220 (924 kJ) ⊙ Fat – 11 g, of which 4 g saturated ⊙ Sodium – 96 mg

1 For the koftas, place the onion, ginger, garlic, and cilantro in a food processor or blender. Puree until blended. Place the ground meat in a bowl and add the blended mixture, spices, and cornstarch. Knead to mix. Cover and refrigerate for 10–15 minutes, for the spices to infuse.

2 For the sauce, heat the oil in a heavy pan, add the onion, and fry gently for 5 minutes. Add the cumin and cardamoms and cook for about 2 minutes, until the onions are browned, then add the garlic and ginger paste and remaining spices. Cook, adding a little water when necessary, for about 5 minutes, until the spices darken. Add the tomatoes and yogurt, stirring continuously.

3 Meanwhile, divide the kofta mixture into 16 equal portions and roll each portion into a smooth round ball. Broil the koftas under a preheated medium broiler for 10 minutes, turning once to drain off all the excess fat.

4 Add the koftas to the sauce mixture. Cook, stirring, for about 2 minutes, then add the water, cover, and simmer for 20–25 minutes. Stir in the chopped chili and cilantro, adding a little boiling water if necessary. Serve with basmati rice and Indian-spiced Mushroom and Pea Sauté (see page 50) if you like.

1 small onion, chopped

2 teaspoons grated fresh ginger root

3 garlic cloves, roughly chopped

3 tablespoons fresh cilantro leaves

11 oz lean ground lamb or beef (about 1½ cups)

½ teaspoon chili powder

¼ teaspoon garam masala

1 tablespoon cornstarch

SAUCE

1 tablespoon vegetable oil

1 small onion, finely chopped

¼ teaspoon cumin seeds

2–3 green cardamom pods

2 teaspoons Ginger and Garlic Paste (see page 123)

½ teaspoon chili powder

¼ teaspoon turmeric

¼ teaspoon garam masala

½ cup chopped tomatoes

1 tablespoon plain yogurt

2 cups water

1 green chili, seeded and finely chopped

2 tablespoons fresh cilantro leaves

bread & spread pudding

Preparation time: 30 minutes
Cooking time: 45 minutes

(V)

Serves 4

NUTRITIONAL FACTS ○ calories – 300 (1254 kJ) ○ Fat – 10 g, of which less than 1 g saturated ○ Sodium – 110 mg

1 Grease a 2½-cup capacity ovenproof dish. Cut the bread into triangles and place a layer in the bottom of the dish. Sprinkle with some of the dried fruit and a little grated orange zest. Continue with these layers, finishing with a layer of bread and spread.

2 In a small pan, heat the milk with the sugar until it just reaches boiling point, then let it cool a little. Add the orange liqueur.

3 Pour the milk mixture over the eggs in a heatproof bowl, whisking to combine. Pour the mixture over the layers of bread and let it soak for about 15 minutes.

4 Sprinkle a little sugar over the top and bake in a preheated 325°F oven for 45 minutes, until the top is puffed up and golden.

a little unsaturated spread, for greasing

5 slices whole-wheat bread, crusts removed, and thinly covered with unsaturated spread

⅓ cup seedless raisins or mixed dried fruit

grated zest of ½ orange

2½ cups skim milk or vanilla soy milk

2 tablespoons sugar, plus extra for sprinkling

splash of Cointreau or Grand Marnier

2 eggs, beaten

NUTRITIONAL TIPS
Boosting soy intake could have a major effect on reducing the incidence of heart disease. Soy milk is made from ground, whole soybeans. It is lactose- and casein-free, and some brands are fortified with calcium, vitamin D, and vitamin B12.

plum charlotte

Preparation time: 20 minutes

Cooking time: 40–45 minutes

NUTRITIONAL FACTS   ○ calories – 255 (1071 kJ)   ○ Fat – 8 g, of which 2 g saturated   ○ Sodium – 220 mg

(V)   **Serves 6**

1 Grease the bottom and sides of a shallow baking dish with a little of the unsaturated spread. Cover the bottom with some of the bread crumbs.

2 Place a layer of plums in the dish, sprinkle with some of the sugar and a little lemon zest and juice. Dot with more spread.

3 Continue with these layers until all the ingredients are used up, finishing with a layer of bread crumbs and dotting with spread.

4 Pour the orange juice over it and bake in a preheated 375°F oven for 40–45 minutes, until the top is golden brown and the plums are tender.

5 Serve right from the baking dish. Serve with low-fat vanilla pudding or plain fromage frais or yogurt, if you like.

3½ tablespoons unsaturated
  spread
6 oz fresh white bread crumbs
  (about 3 cups)
1½ lb ripe plums, cut in half
  and pitted
½ cup soft brown sugar
finely grated zest and juice of
  ½ lemon
1 cup fresh orange juice

apple & fig crumble

Preparation time: 20 minutes   (V)   **Serves 6**

Cooking time: 25–30 minutes

NUTRITIONAL FACTS   ○ calories – 250 (1050 kJ)   ○ Fat – 8 g, of which 1.5 g saturated   ○ Sodium – 75 mg

1 Sift the flour in a large bowl and lightly rub in the unsaturated spread until the mixture forms coarse crumbs. Stir in the sugar.

2 Place the fruit into a 5-cup-capacity ovenproof dish. Add the lemon zest and juice and cinnamon. Spoon the crumble mixture over the fruit and bake in a preheated 350°F oven for 25–30 minutes, until golden brown. Serve warm.

OR YOU COULD TRY...

Other fruit combinations. Always remember to use plenty of fruit—1–1½ lb—and sweeten slightly sour fruit by mixing with sweeter fruit, a little grated zest and juice of an orange, or a variety of dried fruit. Try the following combinations:

○ Plum and blackberry

○ Rhubarb and strawberry

○ Cranberry and apple

○ Pear and black currant

○ Apricot and peach

1 cup whole-wheat plain flour

¼ cup brown sugar

3½ tablespoons unsaturated spread

1 lb cooking apples, peeled, cored, and sliced

6 dried or fresh figs, chopped

grated zest and juice of 1 lemon

1 teaspoon ground cinnamon

NUTRITIONAL TIPS

Figs are high in dietary fiber, low in fat, and offer a non-dairy source of calcium, iron, and magnesium. They are ideal ingredients in baking, and in salads, and make good snacks.

strawberry & fromage frais roulade

Preparation time: 30 minutes
Cooking time: 8 minutes

(V)   **Serves 8**

NUTRITIONAL FACTS   ○ calories – 110 (462 kJ)   ○ Fat – 3 g, of which 0.7 g saturated   ○ Sodium – 34 mg

1 Lightly grease a jelly-roll pan, about 13 x 9 inches. Line with a single sheet of parchment paper to come about ½ inch over the sides of the pan. Lightly grease the paper.

2 In the top of a double-boiler over hot water, beat the eggs and sugar, until pale and thick. Sift the flour, and fold into the egg mixture along with the hot water. Pour into the prepared pan and bake in a preheated 425°F oven for 8 minutes, until golden and set.

3 Meanwhile, place a sheet of waxed paper an inch larger than the jelly-roll pan on a clean damp dish towel. As soon as it's ready, turn out the jelly roll immediately, face down onto the waxed paper. Carefully peel off the lining paper. Roll the cake up tightly with the new waxed paper inside. Wrap the dish towel around the outside and place on a wire rack until cool, then unroll carefully.

4 Add half the strawberries to the fromage frais or yogurt and spread it over the cake. Roll up the cake again and trim the ends. Dust with confectioners' sugar and decorate with a few strawberries. Puree the remaining strawberries in a food processor or blender and serve as a sauce with the jelly roll.

a little unsaturated spread, for
   greasing
3 eggs
generous ½ cup sugar
scant cup flour
1 tablespoon hot water
1 lb fresh or frozen, thawed and
   drained strawberries, or 14 oz
   canned strawberries in
   natural juice, drained
1 cup plain fromage frais
   or yogurt
confectioners' sugar, for dusting

NUTRITIONAL TIPS
This cake is an absolute indulgence yet it is low in fat, the only fat being in the egg yolks. Although the cake is made with 3 eggs, each serving only contains half an egg at the most. Remember that dietary cholesterol has little effect on blood cholesterol in most people; it is saturated fat that increases blood cholesterol.

summer pudding

Preparation time: 30 minutes plus chilling   (V)   Serves 6

NUTRITIONAL FACTS   O calories – 215 (903 kJ)   O Fat – 0.7 g, of which 0.2 g saturated   O Sodium – 270 mg

1 Cut off and discard the crusts from the bread. Line the bottom and sides of a deep, 5–6 cup-glass pudding bowl with the trimmed bread, fitting the pieces together closely and trimming to fit. Reserve enough bread for the top.

2 Place the fruit, except raspberries and strawberries, in a saucepan with the sugar and water. Heat gently, until the juice begins to run from the fruit and the sugar melts. Remove from the heat, add the liqueur and remaining fruit. Drain the fruit through a nylon strainer, reserving the juice. Spoon the fruit into the bread-lined pudding bowl with half the juices, and cover with the reserved bread for the top.

3 Press the top with a weighted saucer (cover the weight with plastic wrap to prevent tainting the pudding). Stand the pudding bowl in a shallow dish to catch any escaping juices, and then refrigerate overnight. Cover and refrigerate the remaining juices separately.

4 To serve, remove the weight and run a blunt-edged knife around the pudding. Invert onto an edged dish, shaking gently to release the pudding. Carefully lift off the pudding bowl. Brush away areas of white bread with the reserved juices. Serve any remaining juices separately. Decorate the pudding with fruit and leaves. Serve with plain yogurt or fromage frais.

10 oz stale medium-sliced white bread (about 10–12 slices)

1¾ lb mixed ripe summer fruits, such as red currants, white currants, black currants, raspberries, strawberries, and cherries, prepared separately

⅓ cup sugar

⅓ cup water

a little liqueur, such as framboise, crème de cassis, or kirsch

extra fruit and fruit leaves, for decorating

plain yogurt or fromage frais, for serving

NUTRITIONAL TIPS

Black currants are not only very high in vitamin C but also one of the highest sources of vitamin E and therefore these small round berries are bursting with antioxidants. Every 5 black currants contain 4 mg of vitamin C and 0.02 mg vitamin E.

lemon ricotta cheesecake with blueberries

Preparation time: 30 minutes
Cooking time: about 1 hour

V

Serves 10

NUTRITIONAL FACTS ○ calories – 177 (744 kJ) ○ Fat – 8 g, of which 4 g saturated ○ Sodium – 124 mg

1 For the crust, mix together the graham crackers, sugar, cinnamon, and spread in a bowl. In a separate bowl, beat the egg white until frothy. Stir into the crumb mixture. Press into the bottom of a 9-inch springform pan. Bake in a preheated 375°F oven for 7–10 minutes, until lightly browned. Let cool.

2 For the filling, place the ricotta and whole eggs in a food processor or blender and blend until smooth. In a bowl, beat together the ricotta mixture, sugar, yogurt, lemon juice and zest, flour, and vanilla extract until well mixed.

3 In a separate bowl, beat the egg whites until soft peaks form, then fold into the cheese mixture. Spread over the crust. Bake in the oven for 50–55 minutes until the center is firm to the touch.

4 Run a knife around the edge of the cake to loosen, and let cool. Remove the sides of the pan, cover the cheesecake, and refrigerate for at least 2 hours or up to 1 day. Just before serving, spread the top with fromage frais and cover with blueberries or other fruit.

1 lb skim ricotta cheese (about 2 cups)
2 large eggs
½ cup sugar
¾ cup plain yogurt
¼ cup lemon juice
grated zest of 2 lemons
2 tablespoons flour
2 teaspoons vanilla extract
2 egg whites
¾ cup plain fromage frais
10 oz fresh blueberries or other soft fruit (about 2⅓ cups)

CRUST
1¼ cups crushed graham crackers
2 tablespoons sugar
1 teaspoon ground cinnamon
1 tablespoon unsaturated spread
1 egg white

mango & pineapple pavlova

Preparation time: 20 minutes

Cooking time: 1 hour

(V)   **Serves 4**

NUTRITIONAL FACTS   ○ calories – 245 (1029 kJ)   ○ Fat – less than 1 g, of which negligible saturated   ○ Sodium – 77 mg

1 Beat the egg whites in a bowl until they are stiff. Fold in 1 tablespoon of the sugar, then gradually beat in the rest of the sugar. The meringue must be glossy and form peaks when spoonfuls are dropped into the bowl. Fold in the black coffee.

2 Line a cookie sheet with a large sheet of parchment paper. Spread out the meringue mixture to form an 8-inch circle. Make a slight hollow in the center of the meringue, then place in a preheated 250°F oven. Bake for 1 hour or until the meringue is crisp. Remove from the oven and let cool on the paper for about 10 minutes before peeling off.

3 When the meringue is cold, fill the hollow in the top with fromage frais. Arrange the mango and pineapple on top, then drizzle the passion fruit seeds and juice over the fruit.

OR YOU COULD TRY...

These other combinations of fruit to fill the pavlova:

- ○ Strawberries and mango
- ○ Raspberries and blueberries
- ○ Cherries and nectarines
- ○ Pineapple and papaya

3 egg whites
3/4 cup sugar
1 teaspoon strong black coffee
1 cup plain fromage frais
1 cup mango, cut-up
1 cup fresh pineapple, cubed
1–2 passion fruits

NUTRITIONAL TIPS
Pavlova, a much-loved meringue dessert, is surprisingly very low in fat because meringue is made from egg white. Use fromage frais instead of high fat cream, and add any variety of fruit that you like. Orange and yellow fruits, such as mangoes and pineapples, are bursting with ACE antioxidant vitamins.

prune & chocolate crunch

Preparation time: 15 minutes
Cooking time: 30 minutes

(V)

Serves 12

NUTRITIONAL FACTS   ❂ calories – 165 (693 kJ) ❂ Fat – 2 g, of which less than 1 g saturated ❂ Sodium – 75 mg

1 Blend the prunes and water in a food processor or blender until almost smooth. Alternatively, mash with a fork.

2 Place the prune puree and the remaining ingredients, except those for the topping, in a large bowl and mix well.

3 Grease a jelly-roll type baking pan. Spread the prune mixture evenly in the pan and bake in a preheated 350°F oven for about 30 minutes. Let cool in the pan.

4 Before the crunch is completely cold, mix together in a bowl the ingredients for the topping, then spread over the crunch. Cut into 12 squares.

1 cup pitted prunes
$\frac{1}{4}$ cup water
a little unsaturated spread, for greasing
1 cup self-rising flour
$1\frac{1}{4}$ cups rolled oats
$\frac{1}{3}$ cup sugar
1 tablespoon cocoa powder

TOPPING
$\frac{3}{4}$ cup confectioners' sugar
2 teaspoons cocoa powder
a little orange juice

NUTRITIONAL TIPS
Cocoa is another source of antioxidant polyphenols, similar to those found in fruit, vegetables, red wine, and tea, and may have heart-health benefits. Unfortunately, it is also very high in fat. Pureed prunes are a perfect fat substitute to use in baking. Just substitute the puree for butter or margarine on an equal cup-for-cup measure. Prunes also provide fiber, iron, potassium, and vitamin A.

pure fruit cake

Preparation time: 15 minutes
Cooking time: 1½ hours

(V) **Makes 12 slices**

NUTRITIONAL FACTS   ○ calories – 218 (916 kJ)   ○ Fat – 2 g, of which less than 1 g saturated   ○ Sodium – 145 mg

1 Grease a 2-lb loaf pan (about 9 x 5 x 3 inches). Place the dates in a saucepan with the measured water and heat gently until they are soft. Remove from the heat and mash with a fork until pureed.

2 Place the date puree in a bowl with ¼ cup water and all the remaining ingredients, except the slivered almonds. Mix together well. Spoon the mixture into the prepared pan and level the top. Sprinkle with slivered almonds.

3 Bake in a preheated 325°F oven for 1½ hours until a skewer inserted into the middle comes out clean. Toward the end of cooking, you may need to protect the top of the cake with foil.

4 Let the cake cool a little in the pan, then turn out and finish cooling on a wire rack.

a little unsaturated spread, for greasing
2 cups pitted dates
1¼ cups water
1¼ cups seedless raisins
scant cup golden raisins
scant cup currants
generous ⅓ cup candied peel, chopped
1⅓ cups whole-wheat flour
1 tablespoon baking powder
1 teaspoon apple pie spice
grated zest and juice of 1 orange or lemon
¼ cup ground almonds
a few slivered almonds, for decorating

banana & raisin bread

Preparation time: 10 minutes

Cooking time: 50 minute–1 hour

(V) Serves 12

NUTRITIONAL FACTS ● calories – 190 (798 kJ) ● Fat – 7 g, of which 2 g saturated ● Sodium – 110 mg

1 Grease a 2-lb loaf pan (about 9 x 5 x 3 inches). Melt the spread in small saucepan over a low heat. Sift the flour, baking powder, baking soda, salt, and cinnamon into a large bowl. Stir in the sugar, mashed bananas, melted spread, raisins, and eggs, and beat for 3 minutes until smooth.

2 Turn the mixture into the prepared loaf pan and bake in a preheated 350°F oven for 50 minutes–1 hour until a skewer pierced into the center comes out clean. Stand the pan on a wire rack to cool slightly before turning out.

3 The fruit bread is much tastier if left to mellow for 2–3 days wrapped closely in foil. It can be served thinly sliced and spread with low-fat cream cheese or made into sandwiches with thinly sliced apple or mashed ripe banana.

1/3 cup melted unsaturated spread, plus a little extra for greasing
1 1/2 cups whole-wheat flour
2 teaspoons baking powder
1/4 teaspoon baking soda
1/2 teaspoon salt
1 teaspoon ground cinnamon
1/3 cup brown sugar
3 very ripe bananas, well mashed
3/4 cup seedless raisins
2 eggs, lightly beaten

NUTRITIONAL TIPS

Research shows that a dietary pattern with more servings of fruit, vegetables, grains, nuts, and beans, with an emphasis on foods that provide potassium, calcium, and magnesium, helps prevent high blood pressure. All fruit and vegetables are good sources of potassium, but particularly bananas, dried fruit, apricots, rhubarb, black currants, legumes, baked beans, beets, corn, mushrooms, spinach, and potatoes.

basic recipes

vegetable stock

Preparation time: 20 minutes
Cooking time: 1 hour 45 minutes
Makes about 3 quarts

3 medium onions, roughly chopped
5 medium carrots, roughly chopped
3 medium leeks, coarsely sliced
3 medium celery sticks, roughly chopped
3 cabbage leaves, sliced
1 head of lettuce, sliced
6 sprigs of flat-leaf parsley with stems, roughly
    chopped
3 sprigs of thyme
1 bay leaf
4 quarts cold water

1 Place all the ingredients in a very large pot or
stockpot. Cover and bring slowly to a boil.
Reduce the heat to a gentle simmer. Skim off
any scum. Simmer very gently, covered, for
1 hour, skimming from time to time. Do not
disturb or move the stock in any way.

2 Strain well through a fine mesh strainer,
being careful not to force any of the ingredients
through the strainer, since this will cloud the
stock. Let cool, then cover and refrigerate.

O fat-free

O Sodium – 90 mg

chicken stock

Preparation time: 10 minutes
Cooking time: 2–3 hours, plus chilling
Makes about 2¼ quarts

3 lb fresh chicken
1 onion, stuck with three cloves
2 carrots, coarsely sliced
2 celery sticks, coarsely sliced
1 head of garlic, cloves separated and unpeeled
6 sprigs of flat-leaf parsley with stems
3 sprigs of fresh thyme
1 bay leaf
about 3 quarts cold water, to cover chicken by
    at least 3 inches

1 Place all the ingredients in a very large pot or
stockpot. Cover and bring slowly to a boil.
Reduce the heat to a gentle simmer. Skim off
any scum. Simmer very gently, partially covered,
for 2–3 hours for a rich stock, skimming from
time to time. Do not disturb or move the stock
in any way.

2 Strain well through a fine mesh strainer,
being careful not to force any of the ingredients
through the strainer, as this will cloud the stock.
Let cool, then cover and refrigerate for several
hours before removing all the solidified fat.

O fat-free

O Sodium – 94 mg

olive vinaigrette

Preparation time: 5 minutes
Makes 1¼ cups

½ cup balsamic vinegar
½ cup lime juice
2 garlic cloves, crushed
3 black olives, pitted
1 tablespoon Dijon mustard
pinch of sugar

1 Place all the ingredients in a screw-top jar, tighten the lid, and shake well. Store in the refrigerator for up to 7 days.

○ calories – 82 (344 kJ)
○ Fat – 3 g, of which less than 1 g saturated
○ Sodium – 800 mg

fruity dressing

Preparation time: a few minutes
Makes about ⅓ cup

2 teaspoons whole-grain mustard
¼ cup balsamic vinegar
1 tablespoon olive oil
1 tablespoon orange or apple juice
freshly ground black pepper

1 Place the whole-grain mustard, balsamic vinegar, olive oil, orange or apple juice, and pepper in a screw-top jar, tighten the lid, and shake well to combine. Store in the refrigerator for up to 7 days.

○ calories – 130 (340 kJ)
○ Fat – 12g, of which less than 2 g saturated
○ Sodium – 166 mg

ginger & garlic paste

Preparation time: 5 minutes
Makes about 8 oz

4 oz fresh ginger root, peeled and cut
    into chunks
4 oz peeled garlic cloves

1 Blend the ginger with the garlic cloves in a food processor or blender with a very little water, to aid blending. Spoon into an airtight screw-top jar and store in the refrigerator for up to 3 weeks. Alternatively, for freezing, place small quantities in a specially reserved ice-cube tray, or spread the paste onto a baking sheet, freeze, then remove the slab and break into pieces. Store in a plastic freezer bag.

○ calories – 184 (773 kJ)
○ Fat – 2 g, of which less than 1 g saturated
○ Sodium – 19 mg

teriyaki sauce

Preparation time: a few minutes
Cooking time: a few minutes
Makes ⅓–½ cup

1 shallot, finely sliced
1 teaspoon minced fresh ginger root
¼ cup rice wine vinegar or sherry
2 tablespoons reduced-salt soy sauce
1 teaspoon honey
2 tablespoons lime or lemon juice
1 teaspoon sesame oil

1 Place the shallot, ginger, vinegar or sherry, soy sauce, honey, and 1 tablespoon lime or lemon juice in a small saucepan over medium heat. Stir in the sesame oil and remaining lime juice and heat through.

O calories – 140 (588 kJ)
O Fat – 3 g, of which less than 1 g saturated
O Sodium – 10 mg

herbed yogurt & cucumber sauce

Preparation time: 5 minutes, plus chilling
Makes 2–3 servings

4 oz grated cucumber (about 1 cup)
1 tablespoon chopped fresh dill weed or mint
1 cup plain yogurt
1 tablespoon lime or lemon juice
freshly ground black pepper

1 Mix the ingredients together, cover, and chill in the refrigerator for about 30 minutes for the flavors to develop, then serve.

O calories – 125 (525 kJ)
O Fat – 2g, of which less than 1 g saturated
O Sodium – 170 mg

tomato salsa

Preparation time: 10 minutes, plus infusing
Makes 8 servings

1 lb (about 3–4 medium) ripe tomatoes, skinned
 and seeded
1 small onion, finely chopped
1–3 green chilies, seeded, and finely chopped
1 tablespoon white vinegar
pinch of sugar
2 tablespoons chopped fresh cilantro or parsley
freshly ground black pepper

1 Finely chop the tomatoes by hand or blend
very briefly in a food processor or blender. Mix
with the remaining ingredients. Leave for
30 minutes for the flavors to infuse. The salsa
will keep for up to 7 days in the refrigerator.

- calories – 115 (483 kJ)
- Fat – 2 g, of which less than 1 g saturated
- Sodium – 50 mg

mango salsa

Preparation time: 10 minutes, plus infusing
Makes 6 servings

1 mango
7 oz ripe tomatoes, skinned, seeded, and
 chopped (about 3/4 cup)
1 green chili, seeded and finely chopped
1 tablespoon chopped fresh mint
1 tablespoon chopped fresh cilantro leaves
juice of 1 lime
1 tablespoon olive oil
pinch of sugar
freshly ground black pepper

1 For the salsa, cut the mango lengthwise
either side of the thin flat central pit. Cut away
the skin from the flesh. Finely chop the flesh
and place in a bowl with the tomatoes.

2 Add the remaining salsa ingredients. Cover,
and refrigerate for at least 30 minutes for the
flavors to infuse. (The salsa will keep for up to
7 days in the refrigerator.)

- calories – 266 (1114 kJ)
- Fat – 13.4g of fat of which 1.8g is saturated fat
- Sodium – trace

index

acknowledgments

Thank you to all at the Family Heart Association, especially Michael Livingston for giving me time to write this book and Gill Stokes who gave me some of her family's favorite recipes. To all at The Conquest Hospital, Hastings, England, my friends and colleagues in The Nutrition and Dietetic Department for their departmental recipes and to Alison Hassell, Senior Dietitian for working with me on "Making Changes." To all in Cardiology, especially Dr. Richard Wray, Cardiologist for his constant support and encouragement, the Cardiac Rehabilitation Team, and all my patients over the years whom I have been privileged to meet and who have taught me so much. To my own dear children, Lottie, Sam, and Tom, for their resilience—it can't be easy having such a "passionate" dietitian for a Mum! Finally, to Jonathan for his love, hours of patience, and help with this book.

THE AUTHOR

Jacqui Lynas (BSc SRD) is a state-registered dietician with a specialist interest in heart-disease prevention. She works for the Family Heart Association and is an acknowledged expert in her field with over 20 years' experience. She is a regular contributor to medical textbooks, journals, and magazines, as well as being a popular speaker at scientific meetings.

Photographic acknowledgments in source order

Getty Images 5 top right, 5 bottom, 9 top, 9 bottom, 15 bottom **Octopus Publishing Group Limited**/David Jordan 17 detail 1/William Lingwood 16 detail 1, detail 2/William Reavell 1, 5 top left, 10 bottom, 12 top, 12 bottom, 13 top, 14 top, 14 bottom, 15 top, 16 detail 3, 16 detail 4, 16 detail 5, 16 detail 6, 17 detail 2, 17 detail 3, 17 detail 4, 17 detail 6, 17 detail 7, 20 top center, 20 top right, 21, 23, 27, 28 top center, 28 top right, 31, 35, 39, 40 top center, 40 top right, 43, 47, 51, 54 top center, 54 top right, 55, 59, 63, 66, 70 top center, 70 top right, 71, 75, 77, 81, 83, 86 top center, 86 top right, 87, 91 95, 99, 100 top center, 100 top right, 103, 107, 108 top center, 108 top right, 111, 115, 117, 121/Simon Smith 17 detail 5. **Science Photo Library** 7 top, 7 bottom.

For Hamlyn

Executive Editor **Nicky Hill**
Editor **Alice Tyler**
Senior Designer **Peter Burt**
Designer **Mark Stevens**
Special Photography **William Reavell**
Home Economist **Louise Blair**
Picture Researcher **Zoë Holterman**
Production Controller **Aileen O'Reilly**